A2 Music Listening Tests

Edexcel

Hugh Benham

and

Alistair Wightman

R· RHINEGOLD
EDUCATION

www.rhinegoldeducation.co.uk

Music Study Guides

GCSE, AS and A2 Music Study Guides (AQA, Edexcel and OCR)

GCSE, AS and A2 Music Listening Tests (AQA, Edexcel and OCR)

AS/A2 Music Technology Study Guide (Edexcel)

AS/A2 Music Technology Listening Tests (Edexcel)

Revision Guides for GCSE (AQA, Edexcel and OCR), AS and A2 Music (AQA and Edexcel)

Also available from Rhinegold Education

Key Stage 3 Listening Tests: Book 1 and Book 2

AS and A2 Music Harmony Workbooks

GCSE and AS Music Composition Workbooks

GCSE and AS Music Literacy Workbooks

Musicals in Focus, Romanticism in Focus, Baroque Music in Focus, Film Music in Focus, Modernism in Focus, The Immaculate Collection in Focus, Who's Next in Focus, Batman in Focus, Goldfinger in Focus

Music Technology from Scratch

Dictionary of Music in Sound

First published 2011 in Great Britain by

Rhinegold Education

14–15 Berners Street

London W1T 3LJ

www.rhinegoldeducation.co.uk

© 2011 Rhinegold Education,

a division of Music Sales Limited

Rhinegold Education has used its best efforts in preparing this guide. It does not assume, and hereby disclaims, any liability to any party for loss or damage caused by errors or omissions in the guide whether such errors or omissions result from negligence, accident or other cause.

You should always check the current requirements of the examination, since these may change. Copies of the Edexcel specification can be downloaded from the Edexcel website at www.edexcel.com.
Telephone: 01623 467467, fax: 01623 450481, email: publication.orders@edexcel.com.

Edexcel A2 Music Listening Tests

Order No. RHG359

ISBN: 978-1-78038-064-3

Exclusive Distributors:

Music Sales Ltd

Distribution Centre, Newmarket Road

Bury St Edmunds, Suffolk IP33 3YB, UK

Printed in the EU

Contents

The authors

Hugh Benham read Music and English at Southampton University, where he was awarded a PhD for his study of the music of John Taverner. He is a chair of examiners for GCE Music, an in-service trainer, church organist and writer, and formerly taught music in a sixth-form college. Hugh has contributed to *Music Teacher* and *Classroom Music* magazines, and is the author of *Baroque Music in Focus* (Rhinegold, 2nd ed. 2010). His other writing includes two books on English church music, including *John Taverner: his Life and Music* (Ashgate, 2003), articles on early music, contributions to *The New Grove Dictionary of Music and Musicians* (2001) and *Die Musik in Geschichte und Gegenwart,* and a complete edition of Taverner for *Early English Church Music.*

Alistair Wightman read Music at Oxford and then York University, where he was awarded a D.Phil for his study of the music of Karol Szymanowski. He has worked in primary, secondary and further education, and is a freelance teacher and writer as well as principal examiner in history and analysis for A level music. His publications include *Writing about Music* (Rhinegold, 2008) and several books and articles devoted to Tadeusz Baird, Karlowicz and Szymanowski, including *Karlowicz, Young Poland and the Musical Fin-de-siècle* (Ashgate, 1996), *Karol Szymanowski: his Life and Music* (Ashgate, 1999) and *Szymanowski on Music: Selected Writings of Karol Szymanowski* (Toccata Press, 1999).

Acknowledgements

The authors would like to thank the consultant Paul Terry and the Rhinegold Education editorial and design team of Harriet Power and Ben Smith for their expert support in the preparation of this book.

Audio tracks

A CD containing recordings of all the extracts for the listening tests in this book is available to buy separately from Rhinegold Education (978-1-78038-123-7, RHG365).

The publisher and authors are grateful to BBC, BIS, Decca, Deutsche Grammophon, Etcetera, Hanssler Classics, Hyperion, Musical Concepts, Philips Classics and Quartz who have granted permission for the use of their recordings.

Introduction

What this book is for

This book is to help you to do as well as you possibly can in the Further Musical Understanding exam for Edexcel A2 Music (Unit 6). Here you will find various listening tests for Section A of the Unit 6 exam, and also advice and specimen questions to help you prepare for Sections B and C.

How to use this book

➢ **If you are taking the exam in 2012**, first use the listening tests labelled '2012' in Section A (pages 9–12 and 28–31). The listening tests labelled '2013' and '2014' will however provide you with additional valuable practice. In Sections B and C, read the general advice and then concentrate on the questions labelled '2012' (pages 40–41).

➢ **If you are taking the exam in 2013**, first use the listening tests labelled '2013' in Section A (pages 13–16 and 32–35). The listening tests labelled '2012' and '2014' will however provide you with additional valuable practice. In Sections B and C, read the general advice and then concentrate on the questions labelled '2013' (pages 40–41).

➢ **If you are taking the exam in 2014**, first use the listening tests labelled '2014' in Section A (pages 17–20 and 36–39). The listening tests labelled '2012' and '2013' will however provide you with additional valuable practice. In Sections B and C, read the general advice and then concentrate on the questions labelled '2014' (pages 40–41).

For the listening tests in Section A, this book contains spaces in which to write your answers, and for the Aural Awareness questions we have provided the necessary skeleton scores. The music that you must listen to in order to answer the Section A questions can be found on the accompanying CD (RHG365), which can be bought separately from Rhinegold Education.

When working through the exercises, you might want to keep to exam conditions as closely as possible, for example by listening to the music for each test the regulation number of times, observing the appropriate lengths of pauses and so on (there's more on this on pages 7–8). But, early on in the course especially, you can use the tests as practice and learning material rather than as pretend exam questions – for example, by listening to excerpts more times than possible in the exam. Try working through some tests a second time once you have had a chance to forget the answers.

Examination requirements

You must read the full examination requirements as set out in the specification (or syllabus) for Edexcel A2 Music. Your teacher will have a copy, but the information can also be accessed from the Edexcel website (www.edexcel.com). **Remember that specifications can change *and* that some requirements are specific to particular years.** It is your teacher's responsibility and yours to know all about the relevant examination requirements.

Examiners' top tips

Apart from as much listening experience as you have time for, and plenty of practice at each type of test, examiners recommend the following:

1. **Learn the correct technical words.** You must know these because they sometimes appear in the questions and should be used in your answers.

> Some sources of information on technical words are given on page 7, in the introduction to Section A.

2. **Read each question thoroughly** and do exactly what it requires. Correct and relevant information gets marks; irrelevant information does not (even if it is true).

3. **Believe your ears!** In listening tests, write about what you actually hear, rather than what you expect to hear.

4. **Note how many marks are available for each question.** For example, if there is a bracketed three (3) after part of a question, this means that three marks are available, and that you will generally need to make three points in your answer.

5. **Avoid getting bogged down,** especially on questions that carry only a single mark. Near the end of your exam, you may have time to return (refreshed) to answers originally left incomplete.

6. **Manage your time carefully.** You have two hours for the Unit 6 exam. Section A is structured for you – you listen to a CD with all the music you need and there are pauses between the excerpts for you to write your answers. For Sections B and C together you will probably have just under an hour and a half. As Section B carries 26 marks, and Section C 36 marks, it is sensible to spend longer on the latter than on the former. There's no hard-and-fast rule, but you might spend 35–40 minutes on the two 13-mark questions that make up Section B, and the remainder of your time (probably some 50–55 minutes) on the extended essay in Section C.

Section A: Aural Analysis

There are two questions – entitled 'Comparison' and 'Aural Awareness' – which are worth 10 and 18 marks respectively (together they make up 28 of the 90 marks for the whole Unit 6 paper).

Comparison question

For comparison questions, you have to identify and comment on musical features from two excerpts, comparing and contrasting them as required. In the exam you will hear each excerpt three times, in the order A, B; A, B; A, B. There will not be a break between A and B, but there will be a pause after each hearing of Excerpt B. The first two pauses will be 30 seconds in length, and the third (during which you complete your answers) will last for 2 minutes.

In comparison questions, be ready to think about the following musical features:

➢ Melody
➢ Rhythm and metre
➢ Harmony
➢ Tonality
➢ Texture
➢ Form (structure)
➢ Instrumental and/or vocal forces.

> Remember especially that 'tonality' usually means 'key' in Unit 6 – not tone quality or anything like that. 'Harmony' refers to individual chords and successions of chords, and is not an alternative term for accompaniment. For further brief comments on these features, see the glossary (page 72) and recent examiners' reports for Edexcel A2 Music. See also the *Dictionary of Music in Sound* (Rhinegold, 2002).

In each comparison question, you will be asked to place the excerpts in their historical, social or cultural context (notably by identifying genres, composers and dates of composition). The excerpts will be taken from a piece (or from two different pieces) that may be unfamiliar to you. The music chosen will, however, be related in some way to one or more of the set works that you study for Section B and/or Section C.

Although this leaves a vast number of possibilities, it does help to suggest a structure for the listening part of the course. If there is a set work by Bach or Stravinsky, for example, you might listen to other music by the composer in question. If you are studying a trio sonata or fugue, it is a good idea to hear other trio sonatas (and similar chamber-music genres) or other fugues.

The more music you hear, the better equipped you will be to name genres, composers and dates. In fact, the only way to do this is to compare what you are trying to identify with what you have previously heard. Listening to music that you don't know and may not like isn't easy – little and (very) often is a good maxim. There's always the chance, if you listen widely and are open-minded, that from time to time you will come across something unexpectedly wonderful!

Aural awareness question

What we have just said applies equally to the aural awareness question, because again you will be asked to comment on the music's context.

In addition, you will be asked in each test to recognise chords and keys, and complete a dictation task (that is, to write down in musical notation something you have just heard played or sung). You will have to listen to only one excerpt of music, which in the exam you will hear five times, with the following pauses: 30 seconds after the first hearing, 1 minute after the second, 1 minute after the third, 30 seconds after the fourth, and 3 minutes after the fifth. To help you with the aural awareness question, there is a single- or two-stave skeleton score of the music.

Aural dictation may come easily to you or you may need a lot of practice, depending partly on how familiar you are with staff notation. It is a skill worth persevering with, apart from anything to do with the exam: for example, it can be very useful to write down musical ideas when there is a risk of forgetting them and when no means of making a recording is available.

Start by working through the dictation examples on pages 21–27. It is easier to begin with these separate, short examples than with the tests that are embedded in longer pieces of music. There are additional dictation tests in *Edexcel A2 Music Listening Tests,* second edition (pages 19–24). Ask your teacher to make up some more if you run out altogether. Why not also try writing your own tests for your friends to do?

To be able to recognise chords and keys is useful in many forms of music-making, including composing and improvising. You may need a lot of practice with it: one good plan is to work or rework the activities in chapter 2 of the AS *Music Harmony Workbook* (Rhinegold, 2008).

Question 1: Comparison (2012)

Test 1   **Tracks 1–2**

The following questions require you to compare and contrast two excerpts of music (which we will call A and B) from the same work. Listen to both excerpts three times in the order A, B; A, B; A, B.

As explained on page 7, Excerpt B should follow Excerpt A without a break each time. There should be a 30-second pause after the first and second hearings of Excerpt B. Allow yourself 2 minutes after the third hearing of Excerpt B in order to complete your answers.

(a)   Name a percussion instrument heard in Excerpt B but not in Excerpt A.

Cymbal (suspended)   (1)

(b)   Contrast the tempo and rhythm of the two excerpts.

Excerpt A is played at a faster tempo than excerpt B. - Allegro vs Adagio.
at opening
Excerpt B makes some use of dotted rhythm, but excerpt A uses many shorter   (2)
repeated notes

(c)   Name the instrument playing the melody in the second half of Excerpt B.
A is steady tempo throughout,   (1)
Bassoon
B much freer

(d)   How do the melodies of the excerpts differ?
A's melodic line actually falls but B's rises
pcns The melody in excerpt B is much more conjunct' than that is excerpt A,
brother polloud making use of longer notes which are more legato. The melodies
wk of excerpt A make greater use of fourths and fifths, are played much...   (3)
B spans 5th, A has wider range   A has trill   A major B min most staccato and are often

(e)   Name the type of multi-movement orchestral work from which these excerpts are taken.
very chromatic but scalic   (1)
Symphony

(f)   Put a cross in the box next to the composer of these excerpts.

☒ **A** Cage   ☒ **B** Pheloung   ☒ **C** Shostakovich   ☒ **D** Stravinsky   (1)

(g)   Suggest a possible year of composition.

1940   (1)

(Total 10 marks)

Test 2   **Tracks 3–4**

The following questions require you to compare and contrast two excerpts of music (which we will call A and B) from the same work. Listen to both excerpts three times in the order A, B; A, B; A, B.

(a)   Name two instruments heard in Excerpt A but not in Excerpt B.

    1. ....

    2. ....   **(2)**

(b)   Give three similarities between the excerpts.

    1. ....

    2. ....

    3. .... **(3)**

(c)   Apart from the texts set, give three differences between the excerpts.

    1. ....

    2. ....

    3. .... **(3)**

(d)   In which of the following time spans were the excerpts composed?

    ☒ **A** 1550–1580   ☒ **B** 1600–1630   ☒ **C** 1650–1680   ☒ **D** 1700–1730 **(1)**

(e)   Put a cross in the box next to the composer of these excerpts.

    ☒ **A** Bach   ☒ **B** Corelli   ☒ **C** Monteverdi   ☒ **D** Sweelinck **(1)**

(Total 10 marks)

Test 3 **Tracks 5–6**

The following questions require you to compare and contrast two excerpts of music (which we will call A and B) from the same work. Listen to both excerpts three times in the order A, B; A, B; A, B.

(a) Contrast the use of voices in these excerpts.

....

....

.... **(3)**

(b) (i) Name a prominent solo instrument heard shortly after the start of Excerpt A.

.... **(1)**

(ii) Name a percussion instrument heard in Excerpt B but not Excerpt A.

.... **(1)**

(c) Indicate whether the statements below are true or false by placing a cross in the appropriate box.

(i) Ostinato is used in Excerpt A. TRUE ☒ FALSE ☒

(ii) Dotted rhythms are used only in Excerpt B. TRUE ☒ FALSE ☒

(iii) The Dorian mode is used in both excerpts. TRUE ☒ FALSE ☒ **(3)**

(d) Put a cross in the box next to the composer of these excerpts.

☒ **A** Bernstein   ☒ **B** Britten   ☒ **C** Shostakovich   ☒ **D** Walton **(1)**

(e) Suggest a possible year of composition.

.... **(1)**

(Total 10 marks)

Test 4   **Tracks 7–8**

The following questions require you to compare and contrast two excerpts of music (which we will call A and B) from different works by the same composer. Listen to both excerpts three times in the order A, B; A, B; A, B.

(a)   Name two instruments heard in Excerpt B but not Excerpt A.

1.   ....

2.   ....   **(2)**

(b)   What effect for strings is used only in Excerpt B?

....   **(1)**

(c)   Compare and contrast the textures of the two excerpts.

....

....

.... **(3)**

(d)   Contrast the rhythm and metre of these excerpts.

....

.... **(2)**

(e)   Put a cross in the box next to the composer of these excerpts.

☒ **A** Berlioz   ☒ **B** Handel   ☒ **C** Mozart   ☒ **D** Schubert   **(1)**

(f)   Put a cross in the box next to the year when this music was composed.

☒ **A** 1744   ☒ **B** 1784   ☒ **C** 1824   ☒ **D** 1864   **(1)**

(Total 10 marks)

Question 1: Comparison (2013)

Test 1   **Tracks 9–10**

The following questions require you to compare and contrast two excerpts of music (which we will call A and B) from the same work. Listen to both excerpts three times in the order A, B; A, B; A, B.

As explained on page 7, Excerpt B should follow Excerpt A without a break each time. There should be a 30-second pause after the first and second hearings of Excerpt B. Allow yourself 2 minutes after the third hearing of Excerpt B in order to complete your answers.

(a)   Name two instruments that are heard only in Excerpt A.

    1.   ....

    2.   ....   **(2)**

(b)   Compare and contrast the textures of the two excerpts.

    ....

    ....

    ....   **(3)**

(c)   Indicate whether the statements below are true or false by placing a cross in the appropriate box.

    (i)   Syncopation is used in Excerpt A.   TRUE ☒   FALSE ☒

    (ii)   The melody in Excerpt A is more disjunct. TRUE ☒   FALSE ☒

    (iii) A cantus firmus is used in both excerpts. TRUE ☒   FALSE ☒   **(3)**

(d)   Suggest a year of composition for these excerpts.

    ....   **(1)**

(e)   Put a cross in the box next to the composer-arranger of these excerpts.

    ☒ **A** Maxwell Davies   ☒ **B** Poulenc`   ☒ **C** Reich   ☒ **D** Vaughan Williams **(1)**

(Total 10 marks)

Test 2   **Tracks 11–12**

The following questions require you to compare and contrast two excerpts of music (which we will call A and B) from the same work. Listen to both excerpts three times in the order A, B; A, B; A, B.

(a)   Name two instruments used in both excerpts. (Note: there are no violins in either excerpt.)

  1.   ....

  2.   ....   **(2)**

(b)   Give two similarities and one difference between the **bass part** of the instrumental introduction in Excerpt B, and the bass part of the introduction in Excerpt A.

  Similarity 1 ....

  Similarity 2 ....

  Difference ....   **(3)**

(c)   Identify one melodic and one rhythmic difference between the **vocal parts** in these two excerpts.

  Melody ....

  Rhythm ....   **(2)**

(d)   Indicate whether the statements below are true or false by placing a cross in the appropriate box.

  (i)   Both excerpts begin in triple time.   TRUE ☒   FALSE ☒

  (ii)   Both excerpts end with the same type of cadence.   TRUE ☒   FALSE ☒   **(2)**

(e)   Put a cross in the box next to the date of composition of this music.

  ☒ **A** about 1660   ☒ **B** about 1700   ☒ **C** about 1740   ☒ **D** about 1780   **(1)**

(Total 10 marks)

Test 3   **Tracks 13–14**

The following questions require you to compare and contrast two excerpts of music (which we will call A and B) featuring the same trumpeter. Listen to both excerpts three times in the order A, B; A, B; A, B.

(a)   For each part of this question, write A or B in the space provided to indicate which excerpt contains the named musical feature.

    (i)   Repeated octave leaps on saxophone ....

    (ii)   Two saxophones in counterpoint ....

    (iii) Highest trumpet note ....

    (iv) Piano part that includes single-line melodic writing ....   **(4)**

(b)   Compare and contrast the use of riffs in the introductory sections of each excerpt (i.e. before the entry of the trumpet).

    ....

    ....

    ....

    ....   **(4)**

(c)   Put a cross in the box next to the term which best describes the jazz style of Excerpt A.

    ☒ **A** Afro-Cuban   ☒ **B** Free   ☒ **C** Swing   ☒ **D** Traditional   **(1)**

(d)   Put a cross in the box next to the decade in which these excerpts were composed.

    ☒ **A** 1910s   ☒ **B** 1940s   ☒ **C** 1970s   ☒ **D** 2000s   **(1)**

(Total 10 marks)

Test 4   **Tracks 15–16**

The following questions require you to compare and contrast two excerpts of music (which we will call A and B) from different works by the same composer. Listen to both excerpts three times in the order A, B; A, B; A, B.

(a)   Indicate by writing A, B or BOTH which excerpts contain the following features:

  (i)   Descending major 7ths ....

  (ii)   Harmonics ....

  (iii)   Repeated melodic tritones ....   **(3)**

> A 'tritone' is an interval encompassing three whole tones. It may be written as an augmented 4th (e.g. C to F♯), or as a diminished 5th (e.g. C to G♭), depending on key and context. In fact the word 'tritone' is conveniently ambiguous; for example you may not always need to say whether augmented 4ths or diminished 5ths (or both) are used in a particular passage.

(b)   Contrast the textures of the excerpts.

   ....

   ....

   ....   **(3)**

(c)   In Excerpt A, the clarinet and violin are both instructed to produce sounds 'like a bird'. Identify two features in this excerpt that suggest birdsong.

  1.   ....

  2.   ....   **(2)**

(d)   Put a cross in the box next to the composer of these excerpts.

   ☒ **A** Debussy   ☒ **B** Goldsmith   ☒ **C** Messiaen   ☒ **D** Poulenc   **(1)**

(e)   Put a cross in the box next to the decade in which these excerpts were composed.

   ☒ **A** 1910s   ☒ **B** 1940s   ☒ **C** 1970s   ☒ **D** 2000s   **(1)**

(Total 10 marks)

Question 1: Comparison (2014)

Test 1   **Tracks 17–18**

The following questions require you to compare and contrast two excerpts of music (which we will call A and B) from different works by the same composer. Listen to both excerpts three times in the order A, B; A, B; A, B.

As explained on page 7, Excerpt B should follow Excerpt A without a break each time. There should be a 30-second pause after the first and second hearings of Excerpt B. Allow yourself 2 minutes after the third hearing of Excerpt B in order to complete your answers.

(a)   What technique is used by the harpist in Excerpt A but not in Excerpt B?

       ....   **(1)**

(b)   Name the type of scale played on the harp when it first enters in Excerpt A.

       ....   **(1)**

(c)   Contrast the melodic writing of the two excerpts.

       ....

       ....

       .... **(3)**

(d)   Name two instruments heard in Excerpt A but not in Excerpt B.

       1.   ....

       2.   ....   **(2)**

(e)   Put a cross in the box next to the term which best describes the style of both excerpts.

       ☒ **A** Expressionist   ☒ **B** Impressionist   ☒ **C** Neoclassical   ☒ **D** Romantic   **(1)**

(f)   Put a cross in the box next to the composer of these excerpts.

       ☒ **A** Debussy   ☒ **B** Poulenc   ☒ **C** Wagner   ☒ **D** Webern   **(1)**

(g)   Put a cross in the box next to the decade in which these excerpts were composed.

       ☒ **A** 1880s   ☒ **B** 1910s   ☒ **C** 1940s   ☒ **D** 1970s   **(1)**

(Total 10 marks)

Test 2   **Tracks 19–20**

The following questions require you to compare and contrast two excerpts of music (which we will call A and B) from different works by the same composer. Listen to both excerpts three times in the order A, B; A, B; A, B.

(a)   Where are these two excerpts most likely to be performed?

....   **(1)**

(b)   (i)   Explain how the texture changes in the course of Excerpt A.

....

....

....   **(3)**

(ii)   Name one way in which the texture of Excerpt B is:

Similar to Excerpt A ....

Different from Excerpt A ....   **(2)**

(c)   Give two ways in which the melodic lines at the start of Excerpt B differ from those of Excerpt A.

....

....   **(2)**

(d)   Put a cross in the box next to the time span in which this music was first published.

☒ **A** 1590–1610   ☒ **B** 1620–1640   ☒ **C** 1650–1670   ☒ **D** 1680–1700   **(1)**

(e)   Put a cross in the box next to the composer of these excerpts.

☒ **A** Byrd   ☒ **B** Gabrieli   ☒ **C** Purcell   ☒ **D** Schütz   **(1)**

(Total 10 marks)

Test 3   **Tracks 21–22**

The following questions require you to compare and contrast two excerpts of music (which we will call A and B) from the same work. Listen to both excerpts three times in the order A, B; A, B; A, B.

(a) What is unusual about the instrumentation at the opening of Excerpt A?

.... **(1)**

(b) In Excerpt B, which two of the following instruments do you hear first? Cello, double bass, flute, clarinet, bassoon. (Note: these two instruments are separated by a gong stroke.)

   1.   ....

   2.   ....   **(2)**

(c) Compare and contrast tempo, metre and rhythm in the two excerpts.

....

.... **(2)**

(d) Give one similarity and one difference between the two excerpts in terms of melodic writing.

   Similarity ....

   Difference .... **(2)**

(e) Put a cross in the box next to the term which best describes the style of both excerpts.

   ☒ **A** Expressionist   ☒ **B** Impressionist   ☒ **C** Romantic   ☒ **D** Serial   **(1)**

(f) Put a cross in the box next to the composer of these excerpts.

   ☒ **A** Berg   ☒ **B** Debussy   ☒ **C** Stravinsky   ☒ **D** Wagner   **(1)**

(g) Put a cross in the box next to the year in which these excerpts were composed.

   ☒ **A** 1875   ☒ **B** 1895   ☒ **C** 1915   ☒ **D** 1935   **(1)**

(Total 10 marks)

Test 4   **Tracks 23–24**

The following questions require you to compare and contrast two excerpts of music (which we will call A and B) from different works by the same composer. Listen to both excerpts three times in the order A, B; A, B; A, B.

(a)   Compare and contrast the textures of the two excerpts.

....

....

....

.... **(4)**

(b)   Give three ways in which the melody of Excerpt B differs from that of Excerpt A.

1.   ....

2.   ....

3.   .... **(3)**

(c)   Comment on how the performer uses the piano's pedals in Excerpt B.

.... **(1)**

(d)   Put a cross in the box next to the composer of these excerpts.

☒ **A** Bach   ☒ **B** Beethoven   ☒ **C** Grieg   ☒ **D** Schumann   **(1)**

(e)   Put a cross in the box next to the time-span in which these excerpts were composed.

☒ **A** 1734–1755   ☒ **B** 1784–1805   ☒ **C** 1834–1855   ☒ **D** 1884–1905   **(1)**

(Total 10 marks)

Dictation exercises

The exercises that follow are to help in the early stages of practice by isolating the dictation task from other aspects of Question 2 (Aural Awareness). Nevertheless, to begin getting used to hearing dictation in context, the exercises have a little given material before and after the part(s) you have to complete.

> In a few cases, tests have been very slightly adapted from the original pieces of music, which are identified in the answers section on pages 49–52.

To ease you into the process of dictation, in tests 1–5 we have asked you to supply note values in some places and pitches elsewhere, not both at the same time. Where pitches have to be supplied, the note values are shown; where note values are to be added, the pitches are given.

> Before tackling tests 1–5 you should have worked with more straightforward and shorter examples. Even supplying just one or two missing note values or one or two pitches can be valuable in the very early stages. Try 'self-dictation': hear a melody in your head, or sing it aloud, and try writing it down.

In each of tests 6–21, as in the exam, a passage is left entirely blank, for you to supply both note values and pitches. You are free to experiment and discover what method of working suits you best, but it may help to start with note values and then add pitches (or to work the other way round), rather than try to supply both melody and rhythm at once. The first time you hear a test, it can help just to decide how many notes there are – perhaps by putting a dot over the stave for each note you hear. You might then want to go straight to using conventional notation, but if it helps, start by indicating pitch with letter names (e.g. A, B, C♯, D), or rhythm by using a grid to show where each note comes in relation to the beat or pulse.

> Most tests use the treble clef, like Edexcel's sample question, and as appears likely in future assessments. The bass-clef tests are a reminder that these are not actually excluded by the specification. For additional bass-clef practice, ask someone to play other tests one or two octaves lower, taking care to avoid too many leger lines.

Practicalities

Your teacher, or someone else, can play a test from the answers section on pages 49–52, while you have in front of you the actual test with blank bar(s) from pages 22–27. Tests can be played on the piano or any other suitable instrument. A tempo mark is suggested, but in early practice the music can be played more slowly if necessary. The person playing the test can begin by sounding the tonic chord of the key in which the test starts, but bear in mind that this will not happen in the exam – you must identify the key from the context.

If there is no one at hand to play the tests for you, go to the relevant book page at www.listeningtests.co.uk and download the MP3 files to your computer or iPod. Tests 1–3 and 5 have been recorded twice – the first time considerably slower than the second.

Alternatively, you may be able to access the music for some tests on CDs or from iTunes. This would enable you to hear the underlying harmony, as happens in the exam, but there can be difficulties with this method, such as locating the precise bars you have to work with.

It does not matter in the early stages how many times you hear a test, but as you approach the exam, limit the number of playings to five.

To monitor your progress, each time you do a test, count up the number of pitches and/or the number of note values you get correct, and turn these into a percentage. Regard 40% or more of the total as good progress, and 70% or more as very encouraging.

Where a solution indicates that there are, for example, nine notes to be supplied, you need to reckon on *nine note values and nine pitches.* A 'note' is a single sound: occasionally a 'note' may have to be written as two symbols tied together.

Examiners' top dictation tips

➤ Identify the key at the beginning of each piece of dictation. Does it change as the test goes on?

➤ Some tests require you to add pitches that carry accidentals. Such accidentals are vital – if you miss them out, the notes that should have had them are counted as wrong.

➤ Sometimes a pattern that you need to add can be worked out from one of the given passages. Be alert to the possibility of straight repetition or melodic sequence.

Test 1

Supply the missing note values in bars 2 and 6–7.

Test 2

Supply the missing pitches in bars 2 and 5–6.

Test 3

Supply the missing note values in bars 3–4, and the missing pitches in bars 7–8.

Test 4

Supply the missing note values in bars 3–4, and the missing pitches in bars 6–7.

Test 5

Supply the missing pitches in bars 5–6, and the missing note values in bar 8.

Test 6

Supply the missing notes from bar 5 (last quaver beat) to bar 8 (third quaver beat).

Test 7

Supply the missing notes from bar 2 (fourth quaver beat) to the end of bar 3, and the pitch of the final note (bar 4).

Test 8

Supply the missing notes from bar 2 (second crotchet beat) to the end of bar 3.

Test 9

Supply the missing notes from bar 2 (fourth quaver beat) to the end of bar 6.

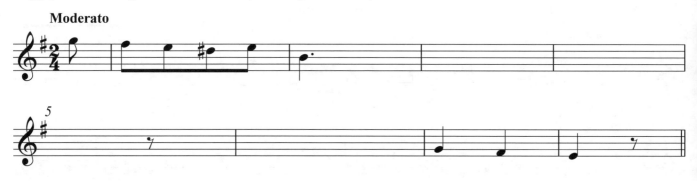

Test 10

Supply the missing notes from bar 2 (second crotchet beat) to bar 3 (first half of fourth crotchet beat).

Test 11

Supply the missing notes from bar 4 (fourth crotchet beat) to bar 7 (first crotchet beat).

Test 12

Supply the missing notes in bars 3 and 4.

> The passage you have to complete includes (like bar 1 and bars 5–7) some triplet quavers.

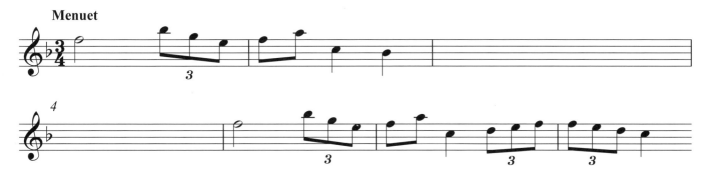

Test 13

Supply the missing notes in bars 4–7.

Test 14

Supply the missing notes from bar 1 (fourth crotchet beat) to bar 3 (second crotchet beat).

Test 15

Supply the missing notes from bar 2 to the start of the third crotchet beat in bar 4.

Test 16

Supply the missing notes from bar 5 (third quaver beat) to the end of bar 7.

Note the large interval at the start – a major 6th. The passage features two other 6ths – one major and one minor.

Non troppo vivace

Test 17

Supply the missing notes from bar 3 (fourth crotchet beat) to bar 5 (first crotchet beat).

Andante

Test 18

Supply the missing notes from bar 1 (last quaver beat) to bar 3 (second crotchet beat).

[Andante]

Test 19

Supply the missing notes in bars 3–4.

Hint: this melody is pentatonic (apart from the short D♭s in bars 1 and 5).

Cantabile

Test 20

Supply the missing notes from bar 3 to bar 7 (second quaver beat).

Andantino sostenuto (ma non troppo)

Test 21

Supply the missing notes from bar 5 (last crotchet beat) to bar 7.

Here's something a little lighter and easier to finish with!

Cheerfully

Question 2: Aural Awareness (2012)

Test 1   **Track 25**

You will hear an excerpt of music five times. The playings will be separated by pauses.

➢   After the first playing, there should be a 30-second pause
➢   After the second playing, there should be a 1-minute pause
➢   After the third playing, there should be a 1-minute pause
➢   After the fourth playing, there should be a 30-second pause
➢   After the fifth and final playing, allow yourself 3 minutes to complete your answers.

There is a skeleton score on page 2 of the score insert, which you must follow as you listen to the music for this test.

(a)   Complete the melody line of bars 54–56. You may work in rough on the skeleton score, but you must copy your answer onto the stave below.

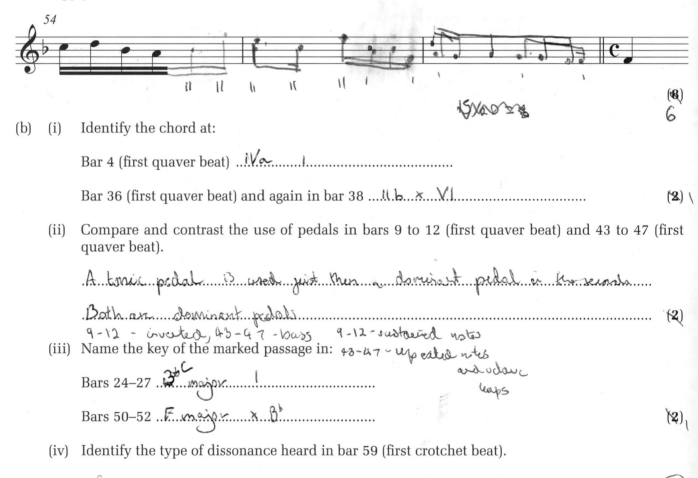

                                                                                                      (8)
                                                                                                        6

(b)   (i)   Identify the chord at:

            Bar 4 (first quaver beat) ..iVa........I.....................................

            Bar 36 (first quaver beat) and again in bar 38 ....II.b...x...VI...........................   **(2)**

      (ii) Compare and contrast the use of pedals in bars 9 to 12 (first quaver beat) and 43 to 47 (first quaver beat).

            A tonic pedal is used just then a dominant pedal in the seconds
            Both are dominant pedals   **(2)**
            9-12 - inverted, 43-47 - bass   9-12 - sustained notes
      (iii) Name the key of the marked passage in: 43-47 - repeated notes
                                                       and octave
            Bars 24–27 ..G major.....I.........................   leaps

            Bars 50–52 ..F major....x..Bb.....................   **(2)**

      (iv) Identify the type of dissonance heard in bar 59 (first crotchet beat).

            ....Suspension...................................   **(1)**
                                                                          Plagagian
      (v)   Identify the type of cadence at the end of the excerpt. ...Imperyet....(plagal).........   **(1)**

(c)   (i)   From what type of work does the excerpt come? ....Concerto grosso.....................   **(1)**

      (ii) Put a cross in the box next to the composer of this music.

            ☒ **A** Berlioz   ☒ **B** Handel   ☒ **C** Haydn   ☒ **D** Mozart (1)

                                                                                   (Total 18 marks)

                                                                                        12

Test 2   **Track 26**

You will hear an excerpt of music five times. The playings will be separated by pauses as indicated on page 28.

There is a skeleton score on pages 3–5 of the score insert, which you must follow as you listen to the music for this test.

(a)   Complete the melody line of bars 41–43. You may work in rough on the skeleton score, but you must copy your answer onto the stave below.

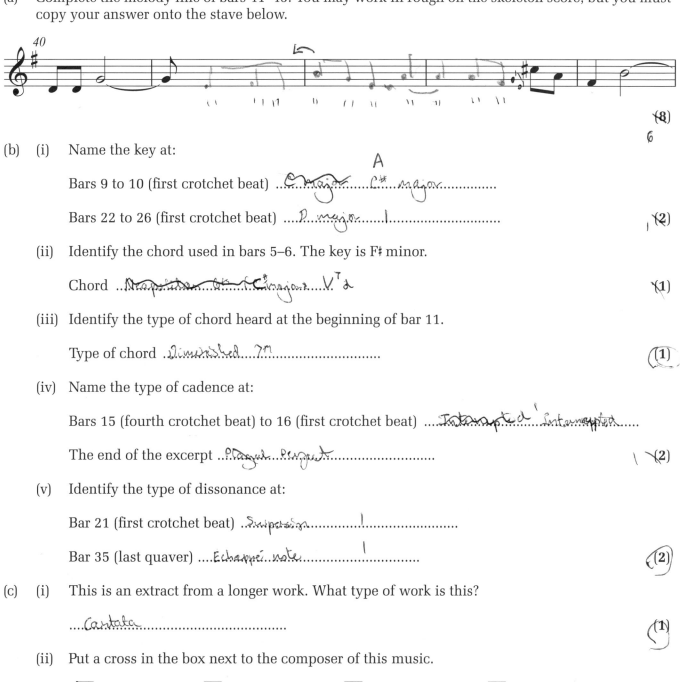

(8)
6

(b)   (i)   Name the key at:

Bars 9 to 10 (first crotchet beat) ..C. maj.... C# major..............

Bars 22 to 26 (first crotchet beat) ....D. major.....|........................   (2)

(ii)   Identify the chord used in bars 5–6. The key is F♯ minor.

Chord ..Napo.....ix....or....C major?....V⁷d   (1)

(iii) Identify the type of chord heard at the beginning of bar 11.

Type of chord ..Diminished...7ᵐ...........................   (1)

(iv) Name the type of cadence at:

Bars 15 (fourth crotchet beat) to 16 (first crotchet beat) ....Interrupted' Interrupted....

The end of the excerpt ..Plagal..Perfect........................ | (2)

(v)   Identify the type of dissonance at:

Bar 21 (first crotchet beat) ..Suspension............|..............

Bar 35 (last quaver) ....Echappé..note.............|.............   (2)

(c)   (i)   This is an extract from a longer work. What type of work is this?

....Cantata...................................   (1)

(ii)   Put a cross in the box next to the composer of this music.

☒ **A** Bach   ☒ **B** Berlioz   ☒ **C** Brahms   ☒ **D** Bruckner   (1)

(Total 18 marks)

13/18

Test 3   **Track 27**

You will hear an excerpt of music five times. The playings will be separated by pauses as indicated on page 28.

There is a skeleton score on page 6 of the score insert, which you must follow as you listen to the music for this test.

(a) Complete the melody line of bars 19–20. You may work in rough on the skeleton score, but you must copy your answer onto the stave below.

(8)

(b) (i)   Through what key does the music pass in bars 4 (third quaver beat) to 5 (first quaver beat)?

....   (1)

(ii) Identify the key in the marked passage from bars 16–17.

....   (1)

(iii) Name the key and type of cadence at the end of the excerpt.

Key ....

Cadence ....   (2)

(iv) Identify the chords in:

Bar 8 (first dotted-crotchet beat) ....

Bar 17 (second dotted-crotchet beat) ....   (2)

(v) What type of chord is heard three times in the marked passage from bars 23–24?

....   (1)

(vi) What type of dissonance is heard at each of the three locations indicated by arrows in bars 10–13?

....   (1)

(c) (i)   The excerpt is from a four-movement sonata. Which movement is it most likely to be from?

....   (1)

(ii) Put a cross in the box next to the composer of this music.

☒ **A** Beethoven   ☒ **B** Corelli   ☒ **C** Mozart   ☒ **D** Shostakovich   (1)

(Total 18 marks)

Test 4   **Track 28**

You will hear an excerpt of music five times. The playings will be separated by pauses as indicated on page 28.

There is a skeleton score on page 7 of the score insert, which you must follow as you listen to the music for this test.

(a)   Write out the melody line of bars 6 (second crotchet) to 8 (third quaver). You may work in rough on the skeleton score, but you must copy your answer onto the stave below.

                                                                                                        (8)

(b)   (i)   Identify the keys and cadences in bars 14 and 24–25.

           Bar 14:   Key ....

                          Cadence ....

           Bars 24–25: Key ....

                          Cadence ....   **(4)**

      (ii)   Identify the key in bar 21.

           ....   **(1)**

      (iii) Name the type of dissonance used in bar 9.

           ....   **(1)**

      (iv)   Precisely describe the harmonic device used in bars 10–12.

           ....   **(1)**

(c)   (i)   From what type of work is this excerpt taken?

           ....   **(1)**

      (ii)   Put a cross in the box next to the composer of this music.

           ☒ **A** Corelli   ☒ **B** Dowland   ☒ **C** Handel   ☒ **D** Purcell   **(1)**

      (iii) Put a cross in the box next to the year in which this music was composed.

           ☒ **A** 1592   ☒ **B** 1642   ☒ **C** 1692   ☒ **D** 1742   **(1)**

                                                                                          (Total 18 marks)

Question 2: Aural Awareness (2013)

Test 1   **Track 29**

You will hear an excerpt of music five times. The playings will be separated by pauses.

➢   After the first playing, there should be a 30-second pause
➢   After the second playing, there should be a 1-minute pause
➢   After the third playing, there should be a 1-minute pause
➢   After the fourth playing, there should be a 30-second pause
➢   After the fifth and final playing, allow yourself 3 minutes to complete your answers.

There is a skeleton score on pages 8–9 of the score insert, which you must follow as you listen to the music for this test.

(a)   Complete the melody line of bars 36–39. You may work in rough on the skeleton score, but you must copy your answer onto the stave below.

                                                                                        (8)

(b)   (i)   Name the type of dissonance used in:

             Bar 4, last quaver beat ....

             Bar 11, third crotchet beat ....   **(2)**

      (ii)   Identify the chords at:

             Bar 14, first minim beat ....

             Bar 18, first minim beat ....   **(2)**

      (iii) Name the type of cadence used in bars 24–25.

             ....   **(1)**

      (iv)   Identify the key of the marked passage in:

             Bars 30–33 ....

             Bars 48–54 ....

             Bars 64–68 ....   **(3)**

(c)   (i)   From what type of work is the excerpt taken?

             ....   **(1)**

      (ii)   Put a cross in the box next to the composer of this music.

             ☒ **A** Bach   ☒ **B** Debussy   ☒ **C** Haydn   ☒ **D** Mendelssohn   **(1)**

                                                                                    (Total 18 marks)

Test 2   **Track 30**

You will hear an excerpt of music five times. The playings will be separated by pauses as indicated on page 32.

There is a skeleton score on pages 10–11 of the score insert, which you must follow as you listen to the music for this test.

(a)   Complete the melody line of bars 50–51. You may work in rough on the skeleton score, but you must copy your answer onto the stave below.

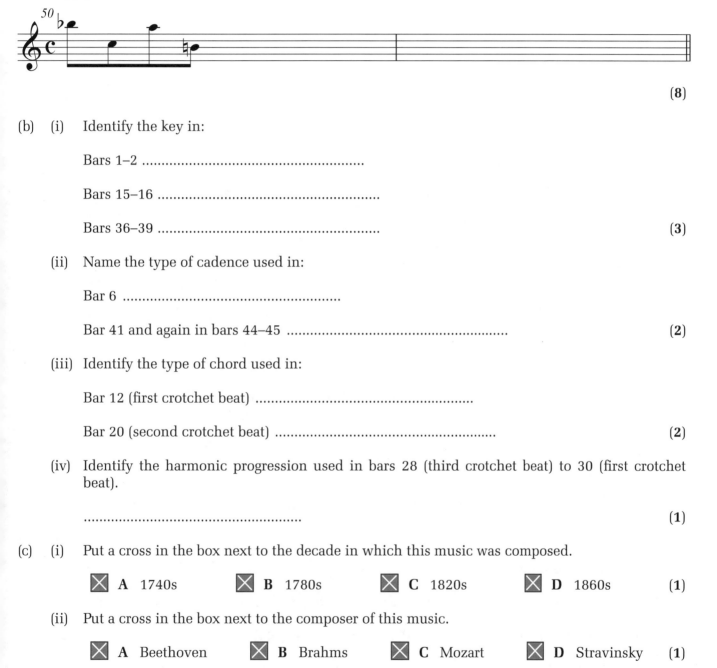

(8)

(b)   (i)   Identify the key in:

            Bars 1–2 ....

            Bars 15–16 ....

            Bars 36–39 ....   **(3)**

      (ii) Name the type of cadence used in:

            Bar 6 ....

            Bar 41 and again in bars 44–45 ....   **(2)**

      (iii) Identify the type of chord used in:

            Bar 12 (first crotchet beat) ....

            Bar 20 (second crotchet beat) ....   **(2)**

      (iv) Identify the harmonic progression used in bars 28 (third crotchet beat) to 30 (first crotchet beat).

            ....   **(1)**

(c)   (i)   Put a cross in the box next to the decade in which this music was composed.

            ☒ **A** 1740s   ☒ **B** 1780s   ☒ **C** 1820s   ☒ **D** 1860s   **(1)**

      (ii) Put a cross in the box next to the composer of this music.

            ☒ **A** Beethoven   ☒ **B** Brahms   ☒ **C** Mozart   ☒ **D** Stravinsky   **(1)**

                                                                                (Total 18 marks)

Test 3   **Track 31**

You will hear an excerpt of music five times. The playings will be separated by pauses as indicated on page 32.

There is a skeleton score on pages 12–13 of the score insert, which you must follow as you listen to the music for this test.

(a)   Write out the melody line of bars 4 (second crotchet beat) to 7. You may work in rough on the skeleton score, but you must copy your answer onto the stave below.

(8)

(b)   (i)   Identify the key at the passage marked in bars 15–17.

....   (1)

      (ii)   Precisely identify the harmonic device in the bass at bars 18–22.

....   (1)

      (iii) Identify the chords indicated in bars 25 and 26.

             Chord A ....

             Chord B ....

             Chord C ....   (3)

      (iv)   Name the type of dissonance used four times in the soprano part of bars 28–29.

....   (1)

      (v)   Identify the key and cadence in bars 33 (third crotchet beat) to 34.

             Key ....

             Cadence ....   (2)

(c)   (i)   Put a cross in the box next to the composer of this music.

             ☒ **A** Beethoven   ☒ **B** Brahms   ☒ **C** Haydn   ☒ **D** Schoenberg   (1)

      (ii)   Put a cross in the box next to the date of composition of this music.

             ☒ **A** 1788   ☒ **B** 1828   ☒ **C** 1868   ☒ **D** 1908   (1)

(Total 18 marks)

Test 4   **Track 32**

You will hear an excerpt of music five times. The playings will be separated by pauses as indicated on page 32.

There is a skeleton score on pages 14–15 of the score insert, which you must follow as you listen to the music for this test.

(a) Write out the melody line of bars 24–25. You may work in rough on the skeleton score, but you must copy your answer onto the stave below.

                                                                                           (8)

(b) (i) Name the type of dissonance that is heard three times in bars 9–11.

         ....

                                                                                           (1)

     (ii) Identify the two chords in bar 36.

         Chord A ....

         Chord B ....

                                                                                           (2)

     (iii) Name the key in bars 41–44, and the type of cadence.

         Key ....

         Cadence ....

                                                                                           (2)

     (iv) Identify the key through which the music passes in:

         Bars 46 to 48 (first crotchet beat) ....

         Bar 62 ....

                                                                                           (2)

     (v) Identify the key at the end of the excerpt.

         ....

                                                                                           (1)

(c) (i) Of what type of piece is this music the beginning?

         ....

                                                                                           (1)

     (ii) Put a cross in the box next to the composer of this music and the approximate date of composition.

         ☒ **A** J. S. Bach, 1730   ☒ **B** Mozart, 1790

         ☒ **C** Mendelssohn, 1830   ☒ **D** Brahms, 1890   **(1)**

                                                                              (Total 18 marks)

Question 2: Aural Awareness (2014)

Test 1   **Track 33**

You will hear an excerpt of music five times. The playings will be separated by pauses.

➢ After the first playing, there should be a 30-second pause
➢ After the second playing, there should be a 1-minute pause
➢ After the third playing, there should be a 1-minute pause
➢ After the fourth playing, there should be a 30-second pause
➢ After the fifth and final playing, allow yourself 3 minutes to complete your answers.

There is a skeleton score on page 17 of the score insert, which you must follow as you listen to the music for this test.

(a) Write out the melody line of bars 11–14. You may work in rough on the skeleton score, but you must copy your answer onto the stave below.

(8)

(b) (i) Identify the key and cadence in bars 24 (third crotchet beat) to 25 (first crotchet beat).

Key ....

Cadence ....   (2)

(ii) Name the key that is visited briefly in bars 18–20.

....   (1)

(iii) Identify the harmonic device used at bar 31, first crotchet beat.

....   (1)

(iv) Identify the chords heard at:

Bar 8 (third crotchet beat) ....

Bar 9 ....   (2)

(v) Identify precisely the dissonance used at bar 22, first crotchet beat.

....   (2)

(c) (i) Put a cross in the box next to the composer of this music.

☒ **A** Bach   ☒ **B** Handel   ☒ **C** Haydn   ☒ **D** Purcell   (1)

(ii) Put a cross in the box next to the year in which this music was composed.

☒ **A** 1651   ☒ **B** 1701   ☒ **C** 1751   ☒ **D** 1801   (1)

(Total 18 marks)

Test 2   **Track 34**

You will hear an excerpt of music five times. The playings will be separated by pauses as indicated on page 36.

There is a skeleton score on pages 18–19 of the score insert, which you must follow as you listen to the music for this test.

(a) Write out the melody line of bars 47–50. You may work in rough on the skeleton score, but you must copy your answer onto the stave below.

                                                            (8)

(b) (i) Identify the key and cadence at the following locations:

         Bars 41–42: Key ....

                          Cadence ....

         Bars 53–54: Key ....

                          Cadence ....   **(4)**

     (ii) Describe the types of chord indicated on the score at the following points:

         Chord A (bar 5, beat 1) ....

         Chord B (bar 33, beat 1) ....

         Chord C (bar 51, beat 2) ....   **(3)**

(c) (i) From what type of work is this excerpt taken?

         ....   **(1)**

     (ii) Put a cross in the box next to the composer of this music.

         ☒ **A** Beethoven   ☒ **B** Brahms   ☒ **C** Mozart   ☒ **D** Wagner   **(1)**

     (iii) Put a cross in the box next to the year in which this music was composed.

         ☒ **A** 1781   ☒ **B** 1811   ☒ **C** 1841   ☒ **D** 1871   **(1)**

                                                                  (Total 18 marks)

Test 3   **Track 35**

You will hear an excerpt of music five times. The playings will be separated by pauses as indicated on page 36.

There is a skeleton score on page 21 of the score insert, which you must follow as you listen to the music for this test.

(a)   Complete the melody line of bars 11–12. You may work in rough on the skeleton score, but you must copy your answer onto the stave below.

                                                                                                  (8)

(b)   (i)   Identify the type of cadence heard in bar 4.

              ....   **(1)**

       (ii)   Identify the key and cadence in bar 6.

              Key ....

              Cadence ....   **(2)**

       (iii) Identify the key in the marked passages from:

              Bars 15–16 ....

              Bars 16–18 ....   **(2)**

       (iv)   Name the type of chord heard in:

              Bar 20 (third and fourth crotchet beats) ....

              Bar 22 (first quaver beat) ....   **(2)**

       (v)   Put a cross in the box next to the word or phrase that describes what happens in bar 8.

              ☒ **A** Augmented 6th chord   ☒ **B** Inverted dominant pedal

              ☒ **C** Suspension   ☒ **D** Tierce de Picardie   **(1)**

(c)   (i)   Put a cross in the box next to the year in which this music was composed.

              ☒ **A** 1732   ☒ **B** 1772   ☒ **C** 1812   ☒ **D** 1852   **(1)**

       (ii)   Put a cross in the box next to the composer of this music.

              ☒ **A** Bach   ☒ **B** Beethoven   ☒ **C** Mozart   ☒ **D** Schumann   **(1)**

                                                                                  (Total 18 marks)

Test 4   **Track 36**

You will hear an excerpt of music five times. The playings will be separated by pauses as indicated on page 36.

There is a skeleton score on pages 22–23 of the score insert, which you must follow as you listen to the music for this test.

(a)   Write out the melody line of bars 26–28. You may work in rough on the skeleton score, but you must copy your answer onto the stave below.

(8)

(b)   (i)   Identify the key and cadence in bars 31–32.

Key ....

Cadence ....   (2)

(ii)   Name the type of cadence in:

Bars 3–4 ....

Bars 7–8 ....   (2)

(iii) Precisely identify the harmonic device used in bars 9–12.

....   (1)

(iv)   Identify the types of chord at:

Bar 20 (third crotchet beat) ....

Bar 36 (third crotchet beat) ....

Bar 45 (third crotchet beat) ....   (3)

(c)   (i)   Put a cross in the box next to the composer of this music.

☒ **A** Beethoven   ☒ **B** Brahms   ☒ **C** Grieg   ☒ **D** Schumann   (1)

(ii)   Put a cross in the box next to the decade in which this music was composed.

☒ **A** 1770s   ☒ **B** 1810s   ☒ **C** 1850s   ☒ **D** 1890s   (1)

(Total 18 marks)

Section B: Music in Context

Section B of the Unit 6 paper deals with the set works for Area of Study 3: Applied Music. You will find the works for the year of your examination listed in the requirements for Unit 6 in the specification.

Section B will contain three questions, of which you have to answer any two. They will be labelled 3 (a), 3 (b) and 3 (c), and each will refer to a different set work. In each case you will be asked to identify particular musical features and indicate how these help to place the piece in its social and historical context.

Answers may be written in note form (bullet points, etc.), in continuous prose, or indeed in some mixture of the two. You may find that use of continuous prose helps you to express your meaning most clearly and fully, and it is a useful preparation for Section C, where this form of writing must be used. Whatever your style of writing, make sure that everything is legible, correct in terms of spelling, punctuation and grammar, intelligible and well organised: you will be assessed on the 'quality of written communication'.

Remember to:

1. Answer the question

    ➢ Include everything that you consider is relevant, even if it seems obvious
    ➢ Avoid everything that is irrelevant, even if it is correct.

2. Give an example if at all possible, whenever you make a point

    ➢ An example nearly always requires a bar reference. For example, if your point is 'The composer uses diminished 7th chords,' add 'as in bar 34, beat 2'. (You will have an unmarked copy of the anthology in the exam to allow you to look up bar references.)

The specimen questions below give you some idea of the way these questions are framed. For sample answers, see page 65.

Additional information on answering this type of question (and Section C questions) is available in the *Edexcel A2 Music Revision Guide* (Rhinegold Education, 2011).

2012

To what extent can the 'Vivo' from Stravinsky's *Pulcinella Suite* (*NAM* 7) be regarded as an example of neo-classicism in music?   **(13)**

2013

What features of *Baris Melampahan* (*NAM* 59) are typical of Balinese gamelan music?   **(13)**

2014

What aspects of melody, harmony and texture in Taverner's *O Wilhelme* (*NAM* 26) help to confirm a date of composition in the first half of the 16th century?   **(13)**

Section C: Continuity and Change in Instrumental Music

Section C of the Unit 6 paper deals with the set works from Area of Study 1: Instrumental Music. Note that these are different from the ones you studied for Unit 3 (at AS level). You will find the works for the year of your examination listed in the requirements for Unit 6 in the specification.

Section C will contain two questions, of which you have to answer only one. They will be labelled 4 (a) and 4 (b). Each option in the specimen Question 4 that was published when the specification was launched deals with three works, and we have assumed in this book that this will be the pattern in the actual exam. Each option in Question 4 will focus on one or more named musical features, asking you to demonstrate how these help us to see continuity and change from one work to another. Discussion will be limited to the named works – it is not necessary to refer to works from outside the anthology.

Answers must be essays written in continuous prose, and quality of written communication will be assessed. As in Section B, make sure that everything is legible, correct in terms of spelling, punctuation and grammar, intelligible and well organised. As your answer will be in essay form, you may wish to include an introductory paragraph and a concluding one, rather than just starting straight in with relevant information as you might in Section B. But to be worthwhile, an introduction or a conclusion must do more than just repeat what is written in the body of the essay.

The specimen questions below give you some idea of the way these questions are framed. For sample answers, see pages 66–69.

2012

Shostakovich: String Quartet No. 8, Op. 110, movement I (*NAM* 9)
Cage: Sonatas and Interludes for Prepared Piano, Sonatas I–III (*NAM* 10)
Corelli: Trio Sonata in D, Op. 3 No 2, movement IV (*NAM* 15)

Compare and contrast approaches to melody, rhythm and metre in the three works listed above. **(36)**

2013

Reich: *New York Counterpoint*, movement II (*NAM* 12)
Holborne: Pavane 'The image of melancholy' and Galliard 'Ecce quam bonum' (*NAM* 13)
Haydn: String Quartet in E♭, Op. 33 No. 2, movement IV (*NAM* 16)

Compare and contrast approaches to tonality and harmony in the three works listed above. **(36)**

2014

Bach: Brandenburg Concerto No. 4 in G, movement I (*NAM* 1)
Beethoven: Septet in E♭, Op. 20, movement I (*NAM* 17)
Debussy: 'Sarabande' from *Pour le piano* (*NAM* 24)

Compare and contrast approaches to structure and texture in the three works listed above. **(36)**

Answers and how to mark them

Note that, in the following mark schemes, letters, words or phrases in parentheses are not essential: for example 'pizz(icato)' means that you get the mark for 'pizzicato' in full or the abbreviation 'pizz.'. Numbers in parentheses are numbers of marks to be awarded. An oblique stroke (/) separates alternative correct solutions. Letters, words or phrases which are <u>underlined</u> are essential: you don't get the mark without them.

If you ever provide *correct and relevant* information that is not listed below – for no mark scheme is completely comprehensive – you can receive credit for this. Ask your teacher if you are in doubt.

Question 1: Comparison (2012)

Test 1

Excerpt A: Shostakovich's Symphony No. 9, Op. 70, movement I
Excerpt B: Shostakovich's Symphony No. 9, Op. 70, movement IV

Dmitri Shostakovich (1906–1975) completed his Symphony No. 9, Op. 70 in 1945 and it received its first performance in November of the same year in Leningrad. Its generally humorous, neoclassical vein caused some consternation, as it was expected that Shostakovich would produce an epic work in the same mould as the seventh and eighth symphonies to celebrate Soviet victory over the Nazis. The first excerpt used here is almost the whole of the exposition from the sonata-form first movement (Allegro), its brevity characteristic of the reduced scale of the work. The darker second excerpt is the opening of the Largo which separates the scherzo and finale.

Related set works: 'Sinfonia', 'Gavotta' and 'Vivo' from Stravinsky's *Pulcinella Suite* (*NAM* 7) – neoclassicism; Berlioz's *Harold in Italy*, movement I (*NAM* 3) – symphony.

(a) (suspended) cymbal (1)

(b) A is quicker/B is slower (1); A is in a steady tempo throughout/B is freer in tempo (1). B makes use of dotted rhythm <u>at the opening</u> (1). Max. 2.

(c) bassoon (1)

(d) A's melodic line initially falls, whereas B's rises (1); A opens with a broken chord followed by a scale, whereas B is mainly conjunct (1); A has a relatively wide range, while B spans only a 5th (1); A contains a trill (1); A is major, whereas B is minor (1). Max. 3.

(e) Symphony (1)

(f) C – Shostakovich (1)

(g) 1945; accept any year between 1920 and 1975 (1)

Test 2

Excerpt A: Monteverdi's *Vespers* (Magnificat, 'Deposuit potentes')
Excerpt B: Monteverdi's *Vespers* (Magnificat, 'Suscepit Israel')

These two excerpts are taken from the Magnificat in Monteverdi's *Vespers* (published in Venice in 1610). Monteverdi was eventually appointed to the post of maestro di cappella at St. Mark's in 1613, and the *Vespers* provide some of the finest examples of the early Baroque concertato style associated with Venetian composers (see Gabrieli's *In ecclesiis*). The excerpts show how Monteverdi combined a sacred cantus firmus (the plainsong melody sung in long notes by the tenor) with the more complex vocal and instrumental elaborations typical of his operatic style.

Related set works: Gabrieli's *In ecclesiis* (*NAM* 27) and Sweelinck's *Pavana Lachrimae* (*NAM* 20) – both dating from the same era. Gabrieli's work is also an example of Venetian concertato music.

(a)   cornett(s) (1); violin(s) (1)

(b)   Both have (essentially) the same (tenor) melody/cantus firmus (1) in long notes (1). The same continuo instruments are used/organ is used in both (1) plus chitarrone/theorbo/large or bass lute (1). Dotted rhythms are used in both (1). Max. 3.

(c)   A has antiphony/dialogue (between cornetts) (1); B has imitation (1). Voices: A has tenor(s)/male voice(s) only *or* B <u>also</u> has sopranos/women's voices (1). Instruments: while A uses (obbligato) instruments/cornetts/violins, B is for (voices and) continuo only (1). A repeatedly uses scales (1). B has (much) melisma (1). Rhythms in B are frequently more complex/florid *or* use shorter/quicker notes (1). Max. 3.

(d)   B – 1600–1630 (1)

(e)   C – Monteverdi (1)

Test 3

Excerpt A: Walton's *Henry V* ('Prologue')
Excerpt B: Walton's *Henry V* ('Agincourt Song' from 'Epilogue')

Walton's score for Olivier's film of Shakespeare's *Henry V* was composed in 1943–44. The first excerpt accompanied the opening shots of medieval London, the passage for wordless chorus underscoring tracking shots of the Thames from the Tower of London to the Globe Theatre (where the play was probably first performed in about 1600). In the epilogue, Walton used a version of the 'Agincourt song' originally composed to celebrate Henry's victory over the French in 1415.

Related set works: Auric's *Passport to Pimlico*: 'The Siege of Burgundy' (*NAM* 42) and Pheloung's *Morse on the Case* (*NAM* 46) – examples of incidental music. Auric's score dates from the same decade as Walton's.

(a)   Excerpt A uses male and female voices *or* B uses male voices <u>only</u> (1). A is wordless/uses vocalisation (1); in B words are sung (1). In A the voices are used purely for colour (1); in B they carry the main melody (1). Max. 3.

(b)   (i) flute (and/or harp) (1); (ii) cymbals (1)

(c)   (i) true (1); (ii) false (1); (iii) false (1)

(d)   D – Walton (1)

(e)   1944; accept any year between 1930 and 1980 (1)

Test 4

Excerpt A: Schubert's String Quartet in D minor ('Death and the Maiden'), movement IV
Excerpt B: Schubert's Octet in F major, movement VI

Both these chamber works were completed in March 1824. The Quartet is known as 'Death and the Maiden' because Schubert used the music from his song of this name as the basis for the variations that form the quartet's second movement. Excerpt B comes from the opening of the finale of Schubert's six-movement Octet. In spite of the dark-toned quality of this excerpt, the Octet as a whole harks back to the relaxed serenade or divertimento style of the mid- to late-18th century. For another example of the genre, see Beethoven's Septet (*NAM* 17).

Related set works: Corelli's Trio Sonata in D, Op. 3 No. 2, movement IV (*NAM* 15) – an example of chamber music; Mozart's Piano Sonata in B♭, K. 333, movement I (*NAM* 22) – an example of an earlier

Viennese Classical style.

(a) clarinet (1), bassoon (1), horn (1), double bass (1). Max. 2.

(b) tremolo (1)

(c) A opens in/has many octaves (1), with chords at the ends of (some) phrases (1). Limited use of imitation (viola and cello) (1). B alternates (1) octaves (1) with homophonic passages (1). Max. 3.

(d) A is in compound duple time ($\frac{6}{8}$) (1); B is in simple quadruple time ($\frac{4}{4}$) (allow any form of simple duple or quadruple) (1). A uses (many) crotchet-quaver/long-short pairs (1); B uses (many) (double-) dotted rhythms (1). Credit additional details. Max. 2.

(e) D – Schubert (1)

(f) C – 1824 (1)

Question 1: Comparison (2013)

Test 1

Excerpt A: Peter Maxwell Davies' *Seven In Nomine*, movement VI
Excerpt B: Peter Maxwell Davies' *Seven In Nomine*, movement II

Peter Maxwell Davies' *Seven In Nomine* originated in a composition exercise undertaken at Princeton University in 1963–64. It is a series of elaborations on the plainsong melody 'Gloria Tibi Trinitas', which was regularly used as a cantus firmus in those English instrumental works from the 16th and 17th centuries known as 'In nomine'. The prototype 'In nomine' was a transcription of the 'in nomine' section from the Mass *Gloria Tibi Trinitas* by John Taverner (d. 1545). Excerpt A, the sixth of the seven *In Nomine*s, is an arrangement of a piece by William Blitheman (d. 1591); it was scored to recreate the sound of a particular chamber organ that Maxwell Davies kept in his studio. In Excerpt B, written in honour of Benjamin Britten's 50th birthday, the plainsong announced on the clarinet is subjected to various transformations, some of which involve octave displacement (compare the clarinet's opening minor 3rd with the 10th heard on the flute).

Related set works: Gabrieli's *Sonata pian' e forte* (*NAM* 14) and Holborne's Pavane 'The image of melancholy' and Galliard 'Ecce quam bonum' (*NAM* 13) – examples of late 16th-century music.

(a) piccolo (1), oboe (1), bassoon (1). Max. 2.

(b) Both open monophonically (1). A moves into a three-part (1) texture with long notes/cantus firmus in the bass/bassoon (1) and (chains of) parallel 3rds/6ths in the upper parts (1). Some dialogue can be heard towards the end (1). B (involves only occasional harmonic structures, and) uses mainly two-part textures (1), though a third part enters near the end (1). Max. 3.

(c) (i) true (1); (ii) false (1); (iii) true (1)

(d) accept any year from 1960 onwards (1)

(e) A – Maxwell Davies (1)

Test 2

Excerpt A: Schütz's *The Christmas Story*, Intermedium I
Excerpt B: Schütz's *The Christmas Story*, Intermedium VIII

Heinrich Schütz (1585–1672) is widely regarded as the most important German composer of his time. Much of his work reflects the influence of the 17th-century Venetian concertato style. *The Christmas Story*, which dates from about 1660, begins and ends with choral movements, between which are eight intermediate pieces ('intermedia' as Schütz called them) for smaller forces. The first (Excerpt A) is a solo in which the Angel addresses the shepherds in the fields. In the last (Excerpt B) the Angel tells Joseph to flee to Egypt with Jesus and his mother to escape the anger of Herod. This movement begins with an example of word-painting, the phrase 'Stehe auf' ('Rise up') being set to an ascending figure.

Related set works: Gabrieli's *Sonata pian' e forte* (*NAM* 14) and Bach's Cantata No. 48, *Ich elender Mensch*, movements I–IV (*NAM* 28). Gabrieli was a Venetian composer known to Schütz, and Bach's cantata is an example of Baroque choral music with German text.

(a)   violas (1); viola da gamba/cello (1); organ (1); (arch)lute/theorbo/chitarrone (1). Max. 2.

(b)   Similarities: ostinato (1) with same two pitches (F–E) (1); four bars long (1). Max. 2. Difference: rhythm reversed/syncopated in B – long note (semibreve), short note (minim) in B instead of short note, long note in A (in both cases beginning on strong beat) (1).

(c)   Melody: at first falling (stepwise) in A but rising (with a leap) in B (1); higher range in A *or* lower range in B (1); some use of recitative style in B (1). Max. 1. Rhythm: more short note values in B (1); Lombardic rhythms/scotch snaps (near end) in B (1); final very long (inverted tonic pedal) note in B (1). Max. 1.

(d)   (i) true (1); (ii) false (1)

(e)   A – about 1660 (1)

Test 3

Excerpt A: Dizzy Gillespie and Gil Fuller's *Manteca*
Excerpt B: Dizzy Gillespie's *A Night in Tunisia*

Dizzy Gillespie (1917–1993), an American trumpeter, composer and bandleader, was associated with bop (or bebop as it can also be termed) in the 1940s and played in a quintet alongside Charlie Parker. He expanded his jazz style by introducing Afro-Cuban rhythms, which are evident in both these excerpts (composed in the late 1940s but heard here in later recordings). A Gillespie trademark from 1954 was a specially-designed trumpet with the bell pointing upwards at an angle of 45 degrees.

Related set work: Miles Davis' *Four* (opening) (*NAM* 50) – bebop-style piece.

(a)   (i) A (1); (ii) B (1); (iii) A (1); (iv) A (1)

(b)   Both excerpts feature a bass riff (1). Additional riffs are as follows: in A, <u>octaves</u> (on saxophone) (1); in B, on vibraphone (1), and on saxophones – one involving triplets followed by a leap (1), and the other involving alternating notes (1). Max. 4.

(c)   A – Afro-Cuban (1)

(d)   Dizzy Gillespie (1)

(e)   B – 1940s (1)

Test 4

Excerpt A: Messiaen's *Quatuor pour le fin du temps*, movement I
Excerpt B: Messiaen's *Turangalîla Symphony*, movement IX

Olivier Messiaen (1908–1992) composed *Quatuor pour le fin du temps* (*Quartet for the End of Time*) while being held in a prisoner-of-war camp in the early 1940s. It reflected his interest in isorhythmic techniques (i.e. the use of recurring sets of rhythmic durations), combined in this work with recurring sets of pitches, both melodic and harmonic. The massive ten-movement *Turangalîla Symphony*, completed in 1948, was according to the composer a 'song of love, hymn to joy, time, movement, rhythm, life and death'. Its title, derived from Sanskrit, refers to time that flies like a galloping horse (*Turanga*) and a game (*lîla*) in the sense of the divine workings of the cosmos, of creation, destruction and reconstruction. The mesmeric ninth movement – 'Turangalîla III' – hints at Messiaen's debt to non-European musical cultures.

Related set works: Gong Kebyar de Sebatu, *Baris Melampahan* (*NAM* 59) – compare the sonorities of this gamelan piece with those of 'Turangalîla III'; Debussy's *Prélude à l'après-midi d'un faune* (*NAM* 5) – modern French music; Goldsmith's *Planet of the Apes:* 'The Hunt' (*NAM* 44) – large-scale orchestration, involving unusual instrumentation.

(a)　(i) B (1); (ii) A (1); (iii) BOTH (1)

(b)　A has piano chords throughout (1) supporting (non-imitative) counterpoint (1) for three instruments (1); B is (largely) monophonic (1), with the melody passing from one instrument to another (1). Max. 3.

(c)　Rapidly repeated notes (1); acciaccaturas (1); trills (1); rhythmically irregular (1) fragmentary lines (1). Max. 2.

(d)　C – Messiaen (1)

(e)　B – 1940s (1)

Question 1: Comparison (2014)

Test 1

Excerpt A: Debussy's *Images pour orchestre* (No. 1, 'Gigues')
Excerpt B: Debussy's *Six épigraphes antiques* (No. 1, 'Pour invoquer Pan, dieu du vent d'été')
(orch. Ernest Ansermet)

'Gigues', the first of Debussy's orchestral *Images*, was completed in 1912. It was intended as a musical evocation of the British Isles, for which reason he incorporated references to the traditional song 'The Keel Row'. This excerpt includes characteristic whole-tone harmonies, and unusually makes use of the oboe d'amore (largely neglected since the 18th century). *Six épigraphes antiques* (1914) was a reworking for piano duet of music composed in 1900–01, to accompany readings of poems based on themes from antiquity by Pierre Louÿs. This version is taken from an orchestration by Ernest Ansermet, conductor of the Suisse Romande Orchestra and a leading interpreter of the works of Debussy, Ravel and Stravinsky.

Related set work: Debussy's 'Sarabande' from *Pour le piano* (*NAM* 24).

(a)　glissando (1)

(b)　whole tone (1)

(c)　A: falling major 3rds (1) making (together with the glissandi) (segments of) a whole-tone scale (1); sequence (1); melody dance-like/(derived from) folksong ('The Keel Row') (1); (later) modal/Aeolian mode (melody in oboe d'amore) (1); grace notes (1). B: (mostly) pentatonic (1); (towards the end) series of falling 3rds (1) spanning a 9th (1). Max. 3.

(d)   celesta (1); cymbal (1); oboe (d'amore) (1); cor anglais (1); side-drum (1). Max. 2.

(e)   B – Impressionist (1)

(f)   A – Debussy (1)

(g)   B – 1910s (1)

Test 2

Excerpt A: Byrd's Mass for four voices ('Gloria')
Excerpt B: Byrd's *Hodie Simon Petrus*

William Byrd (*c*.1540–1623) was the leading English composer of his time. He was a 'recusant': a Roman Catholic at a time when there were severe legal restrictions on and potential penalties for those who did not fully subscribe to the Church of England. Byrd's outstanding musical gifts, patronage from leading Catholic laymen, and the authorities' blind eye did however enable him to enjoy some prosperity. With fellow-recusant Thomas Tallis (*c*.1505–1585), he was even granted a patent for the printing and marketing of part-music and lined music paper by Elizabeth I in 1575. Byrd's output includes much Latin and English church music; among his secular music there are numerous important keyboard works. Neither of our Latin church-music excerpts could have been used openly in England in Byrd's day. The first is from a Mass printed in the early 1590s; the second is one of the motets published in *Gradualia*, part II (1607). It was for an important Catholic feast, that of Sts. Peter and Paul.

Related set works: Taverner's *O Wilhelme, pastor bone* (*NAM* 26) – sacred vocal music in (Tudor and early Jacobean) England; Haydn's 'Quoniam tu solus' from *The Nelson Mass* (*NAM* 29) – Mass (Classical era).

(a)   church/cathedral (1)

(b)   (i) monophony <u>at start</u> (1); four parts (in all) (1), with passages in/reductions to two (1) and three parts (1); imitation (1); antiphony (1). Max. 3.
      (ii) Similarity: imitation/counterpoint (1). Difference: more/six parts/all parts in almost constant use (1).

(c)   major (1) rather than (modal) minor (1); (five-note) rising scalic figure (1) rather than undulating figure (1). Max. 2.

(d)   A – 1590–1610 (1)

(e)   A – Byrd (1)

Test 3

Excerpt A: Berg's *Three Orchestral Pieces* (No. 1)
Excerpt B: Berg's *Three Orchestral Pieces* (No. 3)

Alban Berg (1885–1935), a pupil of Arnold Schoenberg, was a member of the so-called Second Viennese School. His works are sometimes considered rather more approachable than those of Schoenberg or Webern (the other prominent members of the 'school'). They include: the operas *Wozzeck* and *Lulu*; *Kammerkonzert* (Chamber Concerto) for piano, violin and winds; the 'Lyric' Suite for string quartet; and the Violin Concerto, in which Berg fused serial techniques with quotations of Austrian folk music and a chorale by Bach. The excerpts here, from *Three Orchestral Pieces* (1914–15), afford glimpses of his intense and often violent pre-serial expressionist style.

Related set work: Webern's Quartet Op. 22, movement I (*NAM* 8) – a work by another member of the Second Viennese School.

(a)   percussion only (1)

(b)   cello (1); clarinet (1) (in either order)

(c)   A is slow/B is moderately fast *or* in a march tempo (1). In A the pulse is indeterminate *or* time signature is unclear/B is in clear duple or quadruple metre (1). Both use cross-rhythms (1). B uses more repeated rhythmic patterns (1) including dotted patterns (1). Plentiful triplets (*or* tuplets) in A/ occasional (prominent/march-like) triplet figures in B. Max. 2.

(d)   Similarity: (highly) chromatic/atonal/fragmentary lines/some repetition of motifs (1); difference: A is narrower/B is wider in range/B is more active/B has more clearly-defined melodic content (1). Max. 2.

(e)   A – Expressionist (1)

(f)   A – Berg (1)

(g)   C – 1915 (1)

Test 4

Excerpt A: Grieg's *Holberg Suite*, movement IV ('Air')
Excerpt B: Grieg's *Stimmungen* ('Moods'), No. 7 ('Lualåt')

Edvard Grieg (1843–1907) was a Norwegian nationalist composer. His works comprise songs in German, Danish and Norwegian; many short piano pieces ('Lyric Pieces' and folksong arrangements); sonatas for violin and piano, cello and piano and for piano solo – as well as the celebrated piano concerto and incidental music for *Peer Gynt* (a drama by Ibsen). As the extract from the original piano version of the *Holberg Suite* (1884) shows, Grieg anticipated neoclassicism, while the second excerpt (from *Stimmungen*, written in 1898–1905) reveals a kinship with musical impressionism.

Related set works: Sweelinck's *Pavana Lachrimae*, Schumann's *Kinderscenen* (Nos. 1, 3 and 11) and Debussy's *Pour le piano: Sarabande* (*NAM* 20, 23 and 24) – links with Baroque keyboard music, the Romantic miniature and French neoclassicism respectively.

(a)   Both excerpts use melody-dominated homophony (1), and (the harmonic device of) pedals (1). In A (only) melody passes from treble to bass (1). In B there is ostinato (1), and use of drones (1); melody (often) presented in canon (accept imitation instead) (1); monophony at end (1). Max. 4.

(b)   B opens with an octave leap (rather than long repeated notes) (1); simple mordents (rather than more complex/florid/Baroque-style ornamentation) (1); some modal inflections (including flattened 7th and raised 4th) (1); more repetition (rather than sequence) of figures and phrases (1), especially of four-note motif at end (1). Max. 3.

(c)   Sustaining pedal used to blur melodic outlines (1); occasional use of una corda (1). Max. 1.

(d)   C – Grieg (1)

(e)   D – 1884–1905 (1)

Dictation exercises

Test 1

11 note values to be supplied. Starting key: G major. If desired, the tonic chord (G–B–D) can be sounded before one or more playings of the test.

Handel: Minuet from *Alcina,*
bars 9–16

Test 2

12 pitches to be supplied. Starting key: F major. See direction for Test 1 on possible use of tonic chord.

Samuel Wesley:
Gavotte in F, opening

Test 3

7 note values and 6 pitches to be supplied. Starting key: D major.

Mozart: Piano Concerto in D minor,
K. 466, mvt. III, bars 396–403

Test 4

9 note values and 13 pitches to be supplied. Starting key: F major.

Haydn: String Quartet in C major,
Op.33 No. 3, mvt. III, opening

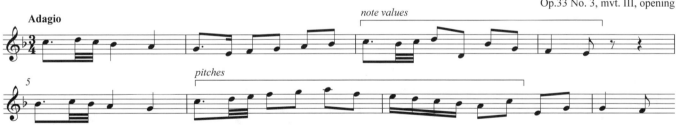

Test 5

9 pitches and 7 note values to be supplied. Starting key: A major.

Schubert: 'Frühlingstraum' from
Die schöne Müllerin, bars 4–14

Test 6

10 notes to be supplied. Starting key: E♭ major.

Beethoven: Quintet in E flat,
Op. 16, mvt. III, bars 8–17

Test 7

9 notes and 1 pitch to be supplied. Starting key: B minor.

Mendelssohn: *Lieder ohne Worte,*
Op. 67 No. 5 in B minor, bars 9–13

Test 8

11 notes to be supplied. Starting key: G major.

Albrechtsberger:
Neue Leichte Praeludien, No. 5, ending

Test 9

12 notes to be supplied. Starting key: E minor.

Schumann: *Album für die Jugend,*
Op. 68 No. 16, ending

Test 10

11 notes to be supplied. Starting key: A major.

Corelli: Sonata in A major,
Op. 5 No. 9, Preludio, opening

Test 11

11 notes to be supplied. Starting key: C minor.

Beethoven: Sonata in C minor,
Op. 13, mvt. II, opening

Test 12

12 notes to be supplied. Starting key: F major.

Haydn: Divertimento (Keyboard Sonata) in F,
Hob. XVI:9, mvt. II, bars 19–25

Test 13

13 notes to be supplied. Starting key: E minor. *Note the diminished 7th chord outline in bars 5–6.*

Vivaldi: Cello Sonata in E minor,
RV 40, mvt. IV, bars 44–54

Test 14

11 notes to be supplied. Starting key: D minor.

Buxtehude: Canzona in D minor,
BuxWV168, bars 66–69

Test 15

12 notes to be supplied. Starting key: D major.

Mendelssohn: *Lieder ohne Worte,*
Op. 85 No 4 in D, bars 20–24

Test 16

9 notes to be supplied. Starting key: C major.

Schubert: 'Halt' from
Die schöne Müllerin, bars 11–19

Test 17

10 notes to be supplied. Starting key: E minor.

Chopin: Nocturne, Op. 72
No. 1, bars 9–13

Test 18

12 notes to be supplied. Starting key: D minor.

Krebs (formerly attrib. J.S. Bach): Fugue from
Prelude and Fugue in D minor, BWV 554, bars 6–9

Test 19

10 notes to be supplied. Starting key: A♭ major.

Vierne: 'Lied' from *24 Pièces en style libre*,
Op. 31, opening

Test 20

11 notes to be supplied. Starting key: E minor.

Reger: 'Elegie' from *Bunte Blätter*,
Op. 36 No. 6, ending

Test 21

12 notes to be supplied. Starting key: E♭ major.

Traditional

Question 2: Aural Awareness (2012)

Test 1

Excerpt: Handel's Concerto in F major, Op. 3 No. 4, movement II

Concerto Op. 3 No. 4 by George Frideric Handel (1685–1759) is classified sometimes as a concerto grosso, sometimes as an oboe concerto, but does not fall readily into any single category. The first movement is a purely orchestral French overture; the second has a part for oboe solo (although it is rarely independent of the first violins); the third employs two oboes, which largely double the violins. Handel's six concerti Op. 3 were published in London in 1734, although much of the music dates from well before this. Op. 3 No. 4, for example, was performed in 1716 at the King's Theatre, Haymarket, London as an 'orchestral concerto' between acts of the opera *Amadigi*.

Related set work: Corelli's Trio Sonata in D, Op. 3 No. 2, movement IV (*NAM* 15) – Baroque music for small ensemble.

(a)

There are 11 pitches and 11 note lengths to complete.

0	No work offered
1	1–3 pitches and/or note lengths correct
2	4–6 pitches and/or note lengths correct
3	7–9 pitches and/or note lengths correct
4	10–11 pitches and/or note lengths correct
5	12–14 pitches and note lengths correct
6	15–17 pitches and note lengths correct
7	18–20 pitches and note lengths correct
8	21–22 pitches and note lengths correct

(b) (i)   bar 4: IV/subdominant (1); bar 36: VI/submediant (1)

(ii)   Both are dominant pedals (in F major/tonic) (1); bars 9–12: inverted/bars 43–47: pedal in bass (1); bars 9–12: sustained note/bars 43–47: repeated notes and octave leaps (1). Max. 2.

(iii) bars 24–27: C major/dominant (1); bars 50–52: B♭ major/subdominant (1)

(iv) suspension (1)

(v)   imperfect/Phrygian (1)

(c) (i)   concerto grosso/orchestral concerto/oboe concerto (1)

(ii)   B – Handel (1)

Test 2

Excerpt: Bach's Cantata No. 80 (*Ein' feste Burg*), movements VI and VII

As cantor to the Thomaskirche in Leipzig, Johann Sebastian Bach (1685–1750) was required to provide a cantata (a multi-sectional vocal/choral work with instrumental accompaniment) for each Sunday and festival day of the church year. His Cantata No. 80, *Ein' feste Burg*, was intended for the Reformation Festivals during the years 1727–1731, and drew on the Lutheran hymn associated above all with the German Protestant Reformation. This excerpt, however, consists of a recitative (a sort of musically heightened speech ['So take thy stand by Jesus' blood-spattered banner'] with continuo accompaniment) that merges with a more lyrical arioso marked by text-repetition ['Salvation now is sure']. The final section is a duet for tenor and alto ['Blessed is he who praises God whose words will sanctify him'], with obbligato parts for oboe da caccia and violin. For a further example of Bach's approach to this genre, see *NAM* 28.

Related set work: Gabrieli's *In ecclesiis* (*NAM* 27) – Baroque sacred music.

(a)

There are 10 pitches and 10 note lengths to complete.

0	No work offered
1	1–2 pitches and/or note lengths correct
2	3–4 pitches and/or note lengths correct
3	5–7 pitches and/or note lengths correct
4	8–10 pitches and/or note lengths correct
5	11–13 pitches and note lengths correct
6	14–16 pitches and note lengths correct
7	17–18 pitches and note lengths correct
8	19–20 pitches and note lengths correct

(b) (i) Bars 9–10: A major (1). Accept instead relative major of dominant (of the recitative's opening and closing B minor) *or* dominant (of the arioso's closing D major). Bars 22–26: D major/dominant (of the duet's opening G major) (1). Accept instead relative major (of the recitative's opening B minor).

(ii) V⁷d/dominant 7th in third inversion (1)

(iii) diminished 7th (1)

(iv) bars 15–16: interrupted (1); end: perfect (1)

(v) bar 21: suspension (with ornamental resolution) (1); bar 35: échappée (1)

(c) (i) cantata/oratorio (1)

(ii) A – Bach (1)

Test 3

Excerpt: Beethoven's Piano Sonata in D, Op. 10 No. 3, movement II

Beethoven's Sonata Op. 10 No. 3 was composed in 1797, not long before the Septet. It forms a fascinating contrast with the latter, indicating that some of Beethoven's most deeply felt earlier works were reserved for the piano. Notice how the melody line is intensified by appoggiaturas, and how the harmonic tension is kept high by the plentiful use of diminished 7th and augmented 6th chords. Keep listening to this excerpt even after you have completed the test, perhaps with a score, to help you become increasingly familiar with the characteristic sounds of these two important types of chromatic chord.

Related set works: Beethoven's Septet in E♭, Op. 20, movement I (*NAM* 17) – music by Beethoven *and* chamber music of the Classical period; Mozart's Piano Sonata in B♭, K. 333, movement I (*NAM* 22) – the piano sonata in the Classical period.

(a)

Accept crotchet E in place of quaver E, quaver rest in second bar above, and/or crotchet C in place of quaver C, quaver rest.

There are 9 pitches and 9 note lengths to complete.

0	No work offered
1	1–2 pitches and/or note lengths correct
2	3–4 pitches and/or note lengths correct
3	5–6 pitches and/or note lengths correct
4	7–9 pitches and/or note lengths correct
5	10–12 pitches and note lengths correct
6	13–14 pitches and note lengths correct
7	15–16 pitches and note lengths correct
8	17–18 pitches and note lengths correct

(b) (i) G minor/subdominant (minor) (1)

(ii) C major/dominant (major) of relative major/relative major of dominant (minor) (1)

(iii) A minor/dominant (minor) (1); perfect (1)

(iv) bar 8: Ic/second inversion of tonic (in D minor/tonic) (1); bar 17: augmented 6th (1)

(v) diminished 7th (1)

(vi) appoggiatura (1)

(c) (i) second/slow (1)

(ii) A – Beethoven (1)

Test 4

Excerpt: 'See, I obey' from Purcell's *The Fairy Queen*

Henry Purcell (1659–1695) was by far the most outstanding English-born composer of the Baroque period. He wrote a good deal of sacred music for the church, but his reputation rests above all on music for the royal court and the theatre. *The Fairy Queen*, first performed at the Queen's Theatre in 1692, is sometimes described as a 'semi-opera'. This is a form partly descended from the courtly 17th-century masque but also influenced by contemporary French opera. Accordingly, and unlike the 'full' opera *Dido and Aeneas*, it does not have music continuously, but combines song, dance and a spoken play (an anonymous adaptation of Shakespeare's *A Midsummer Night's Dream*). The excerpt here is sung by Hymen, the god of marriage, on being summoned to join the festivities.

Related set works: Gabrieli's *In ecclesiis* (*NAM* 27) – 17th-century Baroque vocal music; Corelli's Trio Sonata in D, Op. 3 No. 2, movement IV (*NAM* 15) – late 17th-century music.

(a)

There are 11 pitches and 11 note lengths to complete.

0	No work offered
1	1–3 pitches and/or note lengths correct
2	4–6 pitches and/or note lengths correct
3	7–9 pitches and/or note lengths correct
4	10–11 pitches and/or note lengths correct
5	12–14 pitches and note lengths correct
6	15–17 pitches and note lengths correct
7	18–20 pitches and note lengths correct
8	21–22 pitches and note lengths correct

(b) (i) bar 14: A minor (1), perfect (1); bars 24–25: E minor (1); imperfect/Phrygian (1)

    (ii) G major (1)

    (iii) suspension (1)

    (iv) dominant pedal (1)

(c) (i) accept any of the following: secular/stage-work/opera/semi-opera/masque/ode/cantata (1)

    (ii) D – Purcell (1)

    (iii) C – 1692 (1)

Question 2: Aural Awareness (2013)

Test 1

Excerpt: Mendelssohn's String Quartet No. 1 in E♭, Op. 12, movement I

The string quartet was the leading chamber-music genre in the second half of the 18th century and the first years of the 19th, especially for Haydn and Beethoven. Instrumental chamber music attracted younger composers less, partly because of the growing interest in the relationship of words and music and the consequent development of the German Lied. Some less radical composers continued to compose string quartets, however, including Felix Mendelssohn (1809–1847). At the start of his Quartet in E♭, Op. 12 (1829) Mendelssohn clearly had Beethoven's Quartet in E♭, Op. 74 in mind, as you'll notice if you listen to the beginning of Beethoven's first movement.

Related set works: Haydn's String Quartet in E♭, Op. 33 No. 2, movement IV (*NAM* 16) – string quartet; Brahms' Piano Quintet in F minor, Op. 34, movement III (*NAM* 18) – Romantic chamber music.

(a)

There are 10 pitches and 10 note lengths to complete.

0	No work offered
1	1–2 pitches and/or note lengths correct
2	3–4 pitches and/or note lengths correct
3	5–7 pitches and/or note lengths correct
4	8–10 pitches and/or note lengths correct
5	11–13 pitches and note lengths correct
6	14–16 pitches and note lengths correct
7	17–18 pitches and note lengths correct
8	19–20 pitches and note lengths correct

(b) (i) bar 4: anticipation (1); bar 11: appoggiatura (1)

(ii) bar 14: diminished 7th (1); bar 18: VI/submediant (1)

(iii) imperfect (1)

(iv) bars 30–33: A♭ major/subdominant (1); bars 48–54: G minor/mediant minor/relative minor of dominant (1); bars 64–68: B♭ major/dominant (1)

(c) (i) string quartet (1)

(ii) D – Mendelssohn (1)

Test 2

Excerpt: Mozart's Mass in C minor (K. 427), 'Benedictus'

For Bach, working in Lutheran parts of Germany, the church cantata (with various German words and one or more chorale-based movements) was the principal large-scale sacred genre. In Mozart's Catholic Austria, the Mass (with set Latin texts, including Kyrie and Gloria) enjoyed a somewhat similar status. Mozart's 'Great' Mass in C minor (K. 427), for four soloists, double chorus and orchestra, was composed *c*.1782–83; for unclear reasons it was left unfinished. The existing movements are impressive and some writing is unusually intense: masses in the Classical period were widely indebted stylistically to contemporary light opera, and at various later times have been considered unsuitable for the solemnities of the eucharist.

Related set works: Bach's Cantata No. 48, *Ich elender Mensch*, movements I–IV (*NAM* 28) – multi-movement sacred works from the 18th century; Haydn's String Quartet in E♭, Op. 33 No. 2, movement IV (*NAM* 16) – music of the Classical period.

(a)

There are 10 pitches and 10 note lengths to complete.

0	No work offered
1	1–2 pitches and/or note lengths correct
2	3–4 pitches and/or note lengths correct
3	5–7 pitches and/or note lengths correct
4	8–10 pitches and/or note lengths correct
5	11–13 pitches and note lengths correct
6	14–16 pitches and note lengths correct
7	17–18 pitches and note lengths correct
8	19–20 pitches and note lengths correct

(b) (i) bars 1–2: A minor/tonic (1); bars 15–16: D minor/subdominant (1); bars 36–39: C major/relative major (1)

 (ii) bar 6: imperfect (1); bars 41 and 44–45: interrupted (1)

 (iii) bar 12: augmented 6th (1); bar 20: diminished 7th (1)

 (iv) (Part of) circle of 5ths (1)

(c) (i) B – 1780s (1)

 (ii) C – Mozart (1)

Test 3

Excerpt: Brahms' German Requiem, movement VII ('Blessed are the Dead')

Brahms' German Requiem was completed in 1868 and first performed in Leipzig under Carl Reinecke in 1869; it was very well received, and did much to establish Brahms as a major composer. It was written in memory of Brahms' mother, who had died in 1865. Like some other famous musical settings of the Requiem, it was not intended to form a part of a church service, although it is often performed as a concert work in churches as well as concert halls. Indeed, the title 'German Requiem' indicates that instead of using the traditional Latin words of a Requiem Mass, the texts were assembled from Luther's (Protestant and German) translation of the Bible. The excerpt here is a setting of a passage from the New Testament, from Revelation, chapter 14.

Related set works: Brahms' Piano Quintet in F minor, Op. 34, movement III (*NAM* 18) – the music of Brahms; Bach's Cantata No. 48 (*NAM* 28), *Ich elender Mensch*, movements I–IV – multi-movement sacred works from the German Protestant tradition.

(a)

There are 12 pitches and 12 note lengths to complete.

0	No work offered
1	1–3 pitches and/or note lengths correct
2	4–6 pitches and/or note lengths correct
3	7–9 pitches and/or note lengths correct
4	10–12 pitches and/or note lengths correct
5	13–15 pitches and note lengths correct
6	16–18 pitches and note lengths correct
7	19–21 pitches and note lengths correct
8	22–24 pitches and note lengths correct

(b) (i) G minor/relative minor of subdominant/supertonic minor (1)

(ii) <u>Dominant</u> pedal (1)

(iii) chord A: Neapolitan 6th (1); chord B: Ic/tonic, second inversion (1); chord C: diminished 7th (1)

(iv) suspension (1)

(v) C major/dominant (1); perfect (1)

(c) (i) B – Brahms (1)

(ii) C – 1868 (1)

Test 4

Excerpt: Fugue from Bach's Toccata and Fugue in F, BWV 540

Test 4 is the start of the Fugue from Toccata and Fugue in F, BWV 540 by J. S. Bach (1685–1750). Earlier organ toccatas, including those by Dieterich Buxtehude (1637–1707), tended to juxtapose fugal sections and showy semi-improvisatory passages. Bach's F major Toccata is non-fugal and less obviously showy, but very challenging with its pedal solos, constant semiquaver rhythm and passages of intricate counterpoint. The Fugue begins with a slow-moving subject characterised by an initial chromatic descent. After our excerpt ends, a different, quicker subject is introduced; the piece ends with a masterly combination of the two subjects.

Related set works: Bach's Cantata No. 48, *Ich elender Mensch*, movements I–IV (*NAM* 28) – especially movement I with its complex counterpoint; Brahms' Piano Quintet in F minor, Op. 34, movement III (*NAM* 18) – fugal writing.

(a)

There are 10 pitches and 10 note lengths to complete.

0	No work offered
1	1–2 pitches and/or note lengths correct
2	3–4 pitches and/or note lengths correct
3	5–7 pitches and/or note lengths correct
4	8–10 pitches and/or note lengths correct
5	11–13 pitches and note lengths correct
6	14–16 pitches and note lengths correct
7	17–18 pitches and note lengths correct
8	19–20 pitches and note lengths correct

(b) (i) suspension (1)

    (ii) chord A: V⁷d/dominant 7th, third inversion (1); chord B: Ib/tonic first inversion (1)

    (iii) C major/dominant (1); perfect (1)

    (iv) bars 46–48: B♭ major/subdominant (1); bar 62: G minor/supertonic minor/relative minor of subdominant (1)

    (v) C major/dominant (1)

(c) (i) fugue (1)

    (ii) A – J. S. Bach, 1730 (1)

Question 2: Aural Awareness (2014)

Test 1

Excerpt: 'Happy they' from Handel's *Jephtha*

This excerpt is taken from Handel's final oratorio *Jephtha* (1751), which was based on the story of Jephtha in the Old Testament book of Judges. Jephtha vowed that if victorious in battle he would sacrifice the first living creature he met on his return home. This proved to be his daughter, Iphis, who in Handel's version was spared death through the intervention of an angel. Handelian oratorio was very similar in structure and approach to the opera of the day, though with a larger role for the chorus. 'Happy they' is the brief aria sung by Iphis on her initial acceptance of her fate.

Related set works: Haydn's 'Quoniam tu solus' from *The Nelson Mass* (*NAM* 29) – large-scale choral music of the 18th century; Bach's Brandenburg Concerto No. 4 in G, movement I (*NAM* 1) – music of the late Baroque.

(a)

There are 12 pitches and 12 note lengths to complete.

0	No work offered
1	1–3 pitches and/or note lengths correct
2	4–6 pitches and/or note lengths correct
3	7–9 pitches and/or note lengths correct
4	10–12 pitches and/or note lengths correct
5	13–15 pitches and note lengths correct
6	16–18 pitches and note lengths correct
7	19–21 pitches and note lengths correct
8	22–24 pitches and note lengths correct

(b) (i) F♯ minor/dominant (minor) (1); perfect (1)

   (ii) A major/relative major of dominant (1)

   (iii) tierce de Picardie (1)

   (iv) bar 8: Neapolitan 6th (1); bar 9: V^7d (in B minor) (1)

   (v) 7-6 (1) suspension (1)

(c) (i) B – Handel (1)

   (ii) C – 1751 (1)

Test 2

Excerpt: 'Senta's Ballad' from Act II of Wagner's *The Flying Dutchman*

The Flying Dutchman (*Der fliegende Holländer*) was completed in 1841 and first performed in Dresden in 1843. It is the earliest of Wagner's operas still regularly performed today. Unlike such later works as *Tristan and Isolde* and the *Ring* cycle, this opera still uses individual, largely self-contained numbers (arias, choruses, etc.). It anticipates the later works, however, in its use of leitmotif and subject matter which draws both on legend and the concept of love's redemption. The excerpt is taken from 'Senta's Ballad', in which Senta tells of the fate of the Dutchman and reveals her mounting fascination for him.

Related set work: Wagner's Prelude to *Tristan and Isolde* (*NAM* 4) – 19th-century opera.

(a)

There are 12 pitches and 12 note lengths to complete.

0	No work offered
1	1–3 pitches and/or note lengths correct
2	4–6 pitches and/or note lengths correct
3	7–9 pitches and/or note lengths correct
4	10–12 pitches and/or note lengths correct
5	13–15 pitches and note lengths correct
6	16–18 pitches and note lengths correct
7	19–21 pitches and note lengths correct
8	22–24 pitches and note lengths correct

(b) (i)   bars 41–42: B♭/relative major (1), imperfect (1); bars 53–54: G minor/tonic (1), perfect (1)

      (ii)   chord A: diminished 7th (1); chord B: augmented 6th (1); chord C: Neapolitan 6th (1)

(c) (i)   opera (1)

      (ii)   D – Wagner (1)

      (iii)   C – 1841 (1)

Test 3

Excerpt: Mozart's String Quartet in G, K. 156, movement II

'On the whole, Mozart's early quartets are quite abominable…' So wrote the critic Hans Keller in *The Mozart Companion* (Faber and Faber), which was published in 1956 at the 200th anniversary of Mozart's birth. However, K. 156 was 'a perfect and inspired miniature… a fascinating preview of the great Mozart, and… excellent practice' for performers. (It was composed when Mozart was younger than most A2 Music students.) The intense second movement is both in a minor key and Adagio; for the slow movements of quartets Mozart generally preferred a major key and/or Andante. Our excerpt achieves some of its intensity from the use of diminished 7th chords. How many can you hear in addition to the one that you have to identify in question (b) (iv)?

Related set works: Beethoven's Septet in E♭, Op. 20, movement I (*NAM* 17) – chamber music of the Classical period; Haydn's 'Quoniam tu solus' from *The Nelson Mass* (*NAM* 29) – music of the Classical period.

(a)

There are 11 pitches and 11 note lengths to complete.

0	No work offered
1	1–3 pitches and/or note lengths correct
2	4–6 pitches and/or note lengths correct
3	7–9 pitches and/or note lengths correct
4	10–11 pitches and/or note lengths correct
5	12–14 pitches and note lengths correct
6	15–17 pitches and note lengths correct
7	18–20 pitches and note lengths correct
8	21–22 pitches and note lengths correct

(b) (i)   perfect (1)

   (ii)   G major/relative major (1); imperfect (1)

   (iii) bars 15–16: A minor/subdominant (minor) (1); bars 16–18: B minor/dominant (minor) (1)

   (iv) bar 20: dominant 7th, first inversion/V⁷b (1); bar 22: diminished 7th (1)

   (v)   B – Inverted dominant pedal (1)

(c) (i)   B – 1772 (1)

   (ii)   C – Mozart (1)

Test 4

Excerpt: 'Vanished Days' from Grieg's *Lyric Pieces* (Op. 57)

'Vanished Days' is the first of the six pieces which form the sixth set of *Lyric Pieces* (1893), ten collections of which Grieg published in the course of his career. They are typical short Romantic piano pieces, and as such recall examples by Mendelssohn (*Lieder ohne Worte*), Schumann (*Kinderscenen* and *Waldscenen*) and Brahms (*Intermezzi* and *Ballades*). Grieg's *Lyric Pieces* embrace a variety of styles, some clearly relating to Norwegian folk music. This example, however, illustrates another aspect of his creative character, its melancholy feel conveyed by the poignant falling 7ths and chromatic harmonies.

Related set works: Schumann's *Kinderscenen*, Op. 15, Nos. 1, 3 and 11 (*NAM* 23) – Romantic piano miniatures; 'Sarabande' from Debussy's *Pour le piano* (*NAM* 24) – piano music *c*.1900.

(a)

There are 11 pitches and 11 note lengths to complete.

0	No work offered
1	1–3 pitches and/or note lengths correct
2	4–6 pitches and/or note lengths correct
3	7–9 pitches and/or note lengths correct
4	10–11 pitches and/or note lengths correct
5	12–14 pitches and note lengths correct
6	15–17 pitches and note lengths correct
7	18–20 pitches and note lengths correct
8	21–22 pitches and note lengths correct

(b) (i)   D minor/tonic (1); interrupted (1). Notice that here Grieg replaces the more usual chord VI with an inverted 7th chord. The effect however is still of an interrupted cadence.

     (ii)   bars 3–4: imperfect (1); bars 7–8: perfect (1)

     (iii) dominant pedal (1)

     (iv) bar 20: augmented 6th (1); bar 36: diminished 7th (1); bar 46: Neapolitan 6th (1)

(c) (i)   C – Grieg (1)

     (ii)   D – 1890s (1)

Section B: Music in Context

For Section B and C questions, it is impossible to give a totally comprehensive mark scheme that lists all the possible points that you might make. Instead we have provided for each question what examiners call 'indicative content' – that is, a list of the main relevant points.

In every Section B answer you write, you should illustrate the points made with detailed references to the music under discussion, wherever appropriate. Such references will gain you additional credit. To see how this works, consult Edexcel's indicative content in the Sample Assessment Materials for Unit 6. For example, nine or more relevant points with only limited illustration would be awarded nine or ten marks out of this 13-mark maximum.

Applied Music 2012: Stravinsky

➢ Based directly on a solo cello sonata by 18th-century composer Pergolesi
➢ Rather than pastiche or arrangement, it is what Stravinsky referred to as 'recomposition'
➢ Recomposition achieved through:
  ➢ Novel instrumentation and instrumental techniques, e.g. transfer of cello part to double bass, often in a high register; prominent solo trombone, with glissandi
  ➢ Unusual textures, e.g. heterophony
  ➢ Freer handling of dissonance than in 18th-century music
  ➢ Modified perfect cadences
  ➢ Unexpected stresses/syncopation, emphasised by 'du talon' performance
  ➢ Interpolation of extra bars.

Applied Music 2013: *Baris Melampahan*

➢ Gamelan music requires a large ensemble of performers playing for the most part tuned gongs and metallophones
➢ The instruments are the property of the community rather than of individual members
➢ *Baris Melampahan* is in the modern *gong kebyar* style, with:
  ➢ Alternations of limited musical material
  ➢ Extreme contrasts of dynamics
  ➢ Steady pulse – gongan made up of four-beat *ketegs*
  ➢ Individual parts that remain largely unchanged once established
  ➢ Heterophonic textures
  ➢ A nuclear melody, built on a limited number of pitches from the *pelog* (*selisir*) scale
  ➢ Gongs deliberately pitched slightly differently to produce *ombak* (or 'beat') in tuning.

Applied Music 2014: Taverner

Melody
➢ Mostly conjunct
➢ Relatively narrow range
➢ Leaps usually followed by stepwise movement in opposite direction
➢ Uses major scale/Ionian mode
➢ With a few modal inflections (e.g. E♭ in bar 15)
➢ Mainly syllabic
➢ But melismatic from bar 61.

Harmony
➢ Based chiefly on triads in root position
➢ Avoids on-beat dissonance
➢ More limited harmonic tension from 6ths above bass resolving to 5ths
➢ False relations (notably bar 50⁴–51)
➢ Tierce de Picardie.

Texture
➢ Antiphony
➢ Gymel
➢ Homophony (for clear text projection)
➢ (Imitative) counterpoint near end.

Section C: Continuity and Change in Instrumental Music

In every Section C answer you write, you should illustrate the points made with detailed references to the music under discussion, wherever appropriate. Such reference will gain you additional credit. To see how this works, consult Edexcel's indicative content in the Sample Assessment Materials for Unit 6. For example, 18 or more relevant, well-illustrated points will secure you a mark in the outstanding category (i.e. 32–36 marks), providing of course that you write in continuous prose and that your work is well organised, with a convincing style of writing and few errors in spelling or grammar. In contrast, an essay with a similar number of relevant points without extensive illustration would gain you a mark of between 24 and 27 out of the 30-mark maximum.

Instrumental Music 2012

Melody

Shostakovich:
➢ Often the most prominent part of the texture, thrown into relief by drones
➢ With prominence given to the DSCH motif
➢ Melodies are often chromatic
➢ Appoggiaturas
➢ Much conjunct movement
➢ Narrow-range motifs (including the DSCH figure)
➢ Repetition of motifs
➢ Use of sequence.

Cage:
➢ The usual features of melody are difficult to discern because of preparation/distortion of pitch, etc.
➢ On paper, some apparently chromatic and pentatonic elements
➢ Angular lines.

Corelli:
➢ Combination of conjunct movement with broken-chord figures
➢ Some inversion of main motif
➢ Fragmentation of main motif
➢ Sequence.

Rhythm

Shostakovich:
➢ Generally slow-moving in simple quadruple time
➢ Some long-held drones
➢ Some dotted-crotchet quaver rhythms.

Cage:
➢ Fractal/micro-macrocosmic scheme in which small-scale rhythmic durations determine the overall proportions of the structure
➢ Sonata I uses seven <u>crotchet units</u> in sets of 4–1–3 (repeated); 4–2 (repeated)
➢ These are the rhythmic cells of bars 1–7, amounting to 28 crotchets
➢ Sonata II: $1\frac{1}{2} + 1\frac{1}{2} + 2\frac{3}{8} + 2\frac{3}{8}$ applied to 31 crotchets
➢ Sonata III: $1 + 1 + 3\frac{1}{4} + 3\frac{1}{4}$ applied to 34 crotchets
➢ At surface level, the Sonatas are marked by:
    ➢ Off-beat effects

> ➤ Triplets
> ➤ Other irregular note groupings
> ➤ Rhythmic displacements of short patterns.
➤ III makes use of a more regular pulse
➤ Frequent changes of time signature.

Corelli:
➤ Gigue-like compound duple, involving groups of quavers and semiquavers
➤ Hemiola.

Instrumental Music 2013

Tonality

Reich:
➤ Entirely diatonic
➤ Uses a six-note scale
➤ Which might be compared to B major without D♯, given the five-sharp key signature
➤ But no single tonality emerges clearly (because the harmony is non-functional – see below)
➤ The piece closes inconclusively with E and G♯, implying IV.

Holborne:
➤ Traces of modality persist and characteristic devices include:
> ➤ False relation
> ➤ Tierce de Picardie.
➤ Though not 'functional', the structures are defined by cadences – in the original 'key' and in other closely-related ones
➤ Pavane is (notated) in D major
➤ Galliard is (notated) in D minor.

Haydn:
➤ Clearly defined (and pervasive) E♭ major
➤ Limited modulation to related keys, but with no decisive/structural modulation to the dominant.

Harmony

Reich:
➤ Based on overlapping of chords IV and V
➤ Lacks drive to cadence
➤ Added-note dissonances further obscure tonality.

Holborne:
➤ Mainly root-position chords and first inversions
➤ Second inversion at bar 54 of the Pavane, which is however more of a by-product of the counterpoint
➤ Perfect and imperfect cadences
➤ Pedal points
➤ Suspensions.

Haydn:
➤ Functional progressions, with perfect and imperfect cadences
➤ Perfect cadences frequently preceded by chord II
➤ Besides usual positions of chords and dominant 7ths, there is also a dominant 9th (bars 148–149)
➤ Frequent dominant pedals
➤ Unresolved second inversion at bar 47 (shifts to V⁷ in a different key – F minor).

Instrumental Music 2014

Structure

Bach:
➤ Ritornello.

1–83	Ritornello
83–137	Episode with modulation to D at bar 103
137–157	Shortened ritornello in E minor
157–209	Episode including reference to ritornello opening in A minor
209–235	Ritornello in C
235–323	Episode
323–345	Shortened ritornello in B minor
345–427	Ritornello in G

Beethoven:
➤ Sonata form with slow introduction.

1–18	Adagio introduction
18–111	Exposition
18–39	First subject
40–52	Transition to dominant (B♭)
52–111	Second subject in B♭
111–154	Development, passing through related keys (e.g. C minor, A♭, F minor). Extended dominant preparation leads to…
154–249	Recapitulation, with second subject in dominant
249–288	Coda

Debussy:
➤ Structure can be interpreted as Rondo (see table below) or as Ternary (in which case bars 1–22 are the first A section, 23–41 are B, and 42–62 are a varied repeat of A).

1–8	Section A in C♯ Aeolian
9–14	B
15–22	A¹
23–41	C with tonality blurred by quartal harmony
42–49	A², opening with different harmony (i.e. D major chord)
50–55	D
56–62	B²
63–72	Coda

Texture

Bach:
➤ (Largely) homophonic
➤ With considerable variation of density and layout, e.g. flutes in 3rds, pedal in bass
➤ Some brief use of canon (e.g. bar 235)
➤ Some trio sonata-like textures.

Beethoven:
➢ Texture is highly varied
➢ Melody-dominated homophony, with:
　➢ Some broken-chord accompaniment
　➢ Some syncopation in inner parts.
➢ Chords for varying numbers of parts
➢ Monophony
➢ Octaves
➢ Antiphonal exchange/dialogue
➢ Combination of different themes.

Debussy:
➢ Highly varied texture with:
　➢ Homophony in varying densities/numbers of parts
　➢ Melody-dominated homophony/melody with independent chordal accompaniment.

Remember that credit will be given for describing differences in layout of textures.

Track information by question

Question 1: Comparison (2012)

Test 1: tracks 1–2

Shostakovich: Symphony No. 9, Op. 70, movements I and IV

Belgian Radio and Television Philharmonic Orchestra, Rahbari (cond.)

Shostakovich: Symphony No. 5 / Symphony No. 9 (Naxos 8.550427)

Track 5, 0:00–1:03; track 8, 0:00–1:14

Test 2: tracks 3–4

Monteverdi: *Vespers,* 'Deposuit potentes' and 'Suscepit Israel' from the Magnificat

Scholars Baroque Ensemble

Monteverdi: Vespers of the Blessed Virgin (Naxos, 8.550662–63)

CD2 track 9, 0:00–1:33; CD2 track 11, complete

Test 3: tracks 5–6

Walton: *Henry V,* 'Prologue' and 'Epilogue'

BBC Singers, Trinity Boys Choir, BBC Symphony Orchestra, Leonard Slatkin (cond.)

William Walton: Henry V (BBC MM215)

Track 1, 0:00–1:31; track 10, 4:32–5:38

Test 4: track 7

Schubert: String Quartet in D minor ('Death and the Maiden'), movement IV

Endellion String Quartet

Schubert: Quartet in D minor / Quartet in A minor (BBC MM55)

Track 4, 0:00–0:50

Test 4: track 8

Schubert: Octet in F major, movement VI

Michael Collins (clarinet) and others

Schubert: Octet (BBC MM86)

Track 6, 0:00–1:20

Question 1: Comparison (2013)

Test 1: tracks 9–10

Maxwell Davies: *Seven In Nomine,* movements VI and II

London Sinfonietta, Atherton (cond.)

Peter Maxwell Davies: A Portrait (Decca 475 6166)

CD1 track 14, 0:00–1:19; CD1 track 10, 0:00–1:10

Test 2: tracks 11–12

Schütz: *The Christmas Story,* Intermediums I and VIII

Oxford Camerata, Summerly (cond.)

Schütz: The Christmas Story / Cantiones Sacrae / Psalm 100

(Naxos 8.553514)

Track 2, 0:00–1:13; track 9, 0:00–1:33

Test 3: track 13

Dizzy Gillespie and Gil Fuller: *Manteca*

The Gold Standard Series: Jazz, Big Band and Swing Classics, Vol. 1: Dizzy Gillespie (J2Global)

Track 13, 0:00–1:15

Test 3: track 14

Dizzy Gillespie: *A Night in Tunisia*

Jazz Portraits: Dizzy Gillespie: Small Groups (Saar Srl)

Track 12, 0:00–1:11

Test 4: track 15

Messiaen: *Quatuor pour le fin du temps,* movement I

Amici Ensemble

Messiaen: Quartet for the End of Time / Theme and Variations (Naxos 8.554824)

Track 1, 0:00–1:00

Test 4: track 16

Messiaen: *Turangalîla Symphony,* movement IX

Polish National Radio Symphony Orchestra, Wit (cond.)

Messiaen: Turangalîla Symphony / L'ascension (Naxos 8.554478–79)

CD2 track 2, 0:00–1:00

Question 1: Comparison (2014)

Test 1: track 17

Debussy: *Images pour orchestre,* 'Gigues'

Lyon National Orchestra, Markl (cond.)

Debussy: Orchestral Works, Vol. 3 (Naxos 8.572296)

Track 1, 0:00–1:30

Test 1: track 18

Debussy: *Six épigraphes antiques,* No. 1

Lyon National Orchestra, Markl (cond.)

Debussy: Orchestral Works, Vol. 5 (Naxos 8.572568)

Track 8, 0:00–1:02

Test 2: track 19

Byrd: Mass for four voices, 'Gloria'

Quink Vocal Ensemble

William Byrd: Mass for four voices / Choral music (Etcetera)

Track 2, 0:00–0:49

Test 2: track 20

Byrd: *Hodie Simon Petrus*

The Cardinall's Musick, Andrew Carwood (cond.)

William Byrd: Hodie Simon Petrus (Hyperion CDA67653)

Track 13, 0:00–1:15

Test 3: tracks 21–22

Berg: *Three Orchestral Pieces*, Nos. 1 and 3

South West German Radio Symphony Orchestra, Gielen (cond.)

Mahler / Berg / Schubert (Hanssler Classics 93.029)

CD2 track 2, 0:00–1:30; CD2 track 4, 0:00–1:09

Test 4: track 23

Grieg: *Holberg Suite*, movement IV

Einar Steen-Nøkleberg

Grieg: Piano Music, Vol. 4 (Naxos 8.550884)

Track 4, 0:00–1:13

Test 4: track 24

Grieg: *Stimmungen*, No. 7

Einar Steen-Nøkleberg

Grieg: Piano Music, Vol. 1 (Naxos 8.550881)

Track 17, 0:00–1:19

Question 2: Aural Awareness (2012)

Test 1: track 25

Handel: Concerto in F major, Op. 3 No. 4, movement II

Northern Sinfonia, Creswick (cond.)

Handel: Concerti Grossi Op. 3, Nos. 1–6 (Naxos 8.553457)

Track 14, complete

Test 2: track 26

Bach: Cantata No. 80, movements VI and VII

Nemeth (alto), Mukk (tenor), Hungarian Radio Chorus, Failoni Chamber Orchestra Budapest, Antál (cond)

J. S. Bach: Cantatas, BWV 80 and 147 (Naxos 8.550642)

Track 6, complete; track 7, 0:00–1:01

Test 3: track 27

Beethoven: Piano Sonata in D, Op. 10 No. 3, movement II

Jenö Jandó

Beethoven: Piano Sonatas, Vol. 5 (Naxos 8.550161)

Track 8, 0:00–2:43

Test 4: track 28

Purcell: *The Fairy Queen*, 'See, I obey'

Owen Brannigan, English Chamber Orchestra

Purcell: The Fairy Queen / Dido and Aeneas (Decca 4685612)

CD2 track 4, complete

Question 2: Aural Awareness (2013)

Test 1: track 29

Mendelssohn: String Quartet No. 1 in E♭, Op. 12, movement I

Aurora String Quartet

Mendelssohn: String Quartets, Vol. 2 (Naxos 8.550862)

Track 1, 0:00–2:23

Test 2: track 30

Mozart: Mass in C minor (K. 427), 'Benedictus'

Academy of St Martin in the Fields, Marriner (cond.)

Mozart: Great Mass in C minor (Philips Classics)

Track 12, 0:00–2:13

Test 3: track 31

Brahms: German Requiem, movement VII

Slovak Radio Symphony Orchestra, Rahbari (cond.)

Brahms: A German Requiem (Naxos 8.550213)

Track 7, 0:00–1:54

Test 4: track 32

Bach: Toccata and Fugue in F, BWV 540, Fugue

Walter Kraft

Bach: Complete Organ Music (Musical Concepts 191)

CD5 track 2, 0:00–2:23

Question 2: Aural Awareness (2014)

Test 1: track 33

Handel: *Jephtha*, 'Happy they'

Mona Julsrud, Stavanger Symphony Orchestra

Handel: Jephtha (BIS 1864)

CD2 track 11, 0:00–1:47

Test 2: track 34

Wagner: *The Flying Dutchman*, 'Senta's Ballad'

Austrian Radio Symphony Orchestra, Budapest Radio Chorus, Steinberg (cond.)

Wagner: Der Holländer Fliegende (Naxos 8.660025–26)

CD1 track 13, 0:00–2:53

Test 3: track 35

Mozart: String Quartet in G, K. 156, movement II

Amadeus Quartet

Mozart: The String Quartets (Deutsche Grammophon 001408002)

Track 9, 0:00–2:15

Test 4: track 36

Grieg: *Lyric Pieces*, Op. 57, 'Vanished Days'

Katya Apekisheva

Edvard Grieg: Holberg Suite / Poetic Tone-Pictures / Lyric Pieces (Quartz QTZ2061)

Track 23, 0:00–2:29

Glossary

This glossary is not comprehensive: it refers to terms as used in this volume. For definitions of any common terms relating to tonality and harmony not included here, see the AS Harmony Workbook *and/or the* A2 Harmony Workbook *(Rhinegold Education, 2008). More information on types of dissonance and types of chord is also available in these books. For instruments and fuller definitions of other terms and expressions, consult the* Dictionary of Music in Sound *(Rhinegold Education, 2002).*

Acciaccatura. A very short ornamental note played before a principal melodic note, written or printed as ♪.

Accidental. A symbol that changes the pitch of a note, usually by a semitone.

Aeolian mode. A scale that uses the following pattern of tones (T) and semitones (s): T–s–T–T–s–T–T. When starting on A, it consists of all the white notes within one octave on a keyboard.

Afro-Cuban jazz. A style of jazz that combines **bebop** and Cuban elements, often involving polyrhythm.

Anticipation. A melody note (frequently the tonic of the key in the highest part) sounded slightly before the chord to which it belongs, thereby creating a dissonance with the previous chord.

Antiphony. Performance by different singers/instrumentalists in alternation. Often – but not always – the different groups perform similar material.

Appoggiatura. A non-chord note that sounds on the beat and then resolves by step (up or down a semitone or tone) to the main chord note. The dissonant note is not 'prepared' as a suspension is. Although appoggiaturas are normally approached by leap, accented passing notes that are particularly long and/or prominent are often described as appoggiaturas, even though they are approached by step. Sometimes an appoggiatura, especially in music of the Classical period, is indicated by a note in small type, followed by its resolution printed at normal size.

Aria. A song (usually from an opera, oratorio or cantata) for solo voice, plus accompaniment for orchestra or, sometimes in Baroque times, for smaller forces, even just continuo. An aria often provides a character in an opera with the opportunity to reflect at length on their emotional state.

Arioso. A section or piece that is part way between an **aria** and a **recitative** in the manner of text-setting and level of musical interest.

Augmented 6th chord. A chromatic chord which in root position spans the interval of an augmented 6th, e.g. A♭–F♯.

The chord also includes the major 3rd above the root (and sometimes also the perfect 5th or augmented 4th).

Atonal. Atonal music avoids keys or modes; that is, no pitch stands out consistently in the way the tonic does in tonal music.

Bebop. A style of jazz that developed in the 1940s from swing. More complex and less easy to dance to, it was characterised by improvisation, fast tempos, irregular phrase lengths and a greater emphasis on the rhythm section.

Cadence. A pair of chords signifying the end of a phrase in tonal music. Cadences are of several types, of which perfect and imperfect are by far the most common. *See also* **Imperfect cadence**, **Interrupted cadence**, **Perfect cadence** and **Phrygian cadence**.

Canon. A strict form of imitation, often lasting for a substantial passage or entire piece, where the second part is an exact (or almost exact) copy of the first, even if at a different pitch.

Cantata. Usually a work for voice(s) and instruments in several movements. A cantata is generally shorter than an oratorio, sometimes without chorus, and can be sacred or secular. (In the early 17th century the term cantata (Italian for 'sung') could be applied to more or less any sung piece.) *See also* **Oratorio**.

Chorale. A German hymn of the kind sung in the Lutheran (Protestant) church in the time of J. S. Bach. The word 'chorale' can refer to the words only, or the associated melody only, or to the whole hymn. Chorale melodies are largely stepwise (or conjunct): their harmonisation has long featured in advanced music courses.

Chromatic. A chromatic note is one that does not belong to the scale of the key currently in use. For example, in D major the notes G♯ and C♮ are chromatic. The tonality of a passage containing many chromatic notes may be described as chromatic.

Circle of 5ths. Harmonic progression in which the roots of the chords move by descending 5ths (and/or ascending 4ths), e.g. B–E–A–D–G–C, etc.

Compound time. A metre in which the main beat is subdivided into three equal portions. Opposite of **Simple time**.

Concertato. Concertato style, used mainly in the first half of the 17th century, involved contrasts between different groups of performers, usually both vocal and instrumental.

Concerto. Most commonly, a work for a soloist with orchestra. In many concertos the solo instrument is a piano or violin.

Occasionally there may be two soloists (a double concerto) or even three (a triple concerto). (In the 17th century the term was used more widely, and was applied originally to a work in which voices and instruments, with more or less independent parts, collaborated in a manner that was new at the time.) *See also* **Concerto grosso**.

Concerto grosso. A type of concerto, most common in the late Baroque period, in which three (or occasionally more) soloists, known as the Concertino, are contrasted with the sound of a larger group of mainly string instruments, know as the Ripieno.

Conjunct. Melodic movement by step rather than by leap. Opposite of **disjunct**.

Continuo. Short for 'basso continuo' (Italian for 'continuous bass'), and used chiefly in Baroque music. Refers to an instrumental bassline (most commonly played by cello(s), sometimes with bass(es)), together with an improvised accompaniment on keyboard or lute, which supplies full harmony that might otherwise be lacking.

Contrapuntal. Adjective to describe music that uses **counterpoint**. Counterpoint involves two or more melodic lines (usually rhythmically contrasted), each significant in itself, which are played or sung together – in contrast to **homophony**, in which one part has the melody and the other parts accompany. The term 'polyphonic' is often used as a synonym for contrapuntal.

Counterpoint. *See* **Contrapuntal**.

Cross-rhythm. The use of two or more very different rhythms simultaneously in different parts. One rhythm may imply one metre (or time signature), while another implies a different one.

Dialogue. When two or more instruments or voices have a musical 'conversation', with the individual parts responding to one another.

Diatonic. Using notes that belong to the current key. A diatonic note is one that belongs to the scale of the key currently in use. For example, in D major the notes D, E and F♯ are diatonic.

Diminished 7th. A dissonant four-note chord made up of super-imposed minor 3rds (for example C♯–E–G–B♭).

Disjunct. Melodic movement by leap rather than by step. Opposite of **conjunct**.

Dissonance. Any note not a major or minor 3rd or 6th, perfect 5th, unison or perfect octave above the lowest part sounding is strictly a dissonance. Triads in root position or in first inversion are therefore the only chords that have no dissonance. (Even the 4th above the bass in a second inversion counts as dissonant.) Some dissonances, particularly suspensions and appoggiaturas, add harmonic tension and can help make the music more expressive; others, notably passing and auxiliary notes, provide rhythmic and melodic decoration.

Divertimento. A piece (most commonly from the 18th century) whose style is partly or wholly light and intended to 'divert' or 'amuse' listeners, perhaps at a social function. A divertimento is normally in several movements, with at least one in a dance (particularly minuet) style.

Dominant 7th. A dissonant four-note chord built on the dominant note of the scale. It includes the dominant triad plus a minor 7th above the root.

Dorian mode. A scale that uses the following pattern of tones (T) and semitones (s): T–s–T–T–T–s–T. When starting on D, it consists of all the white notes within one octave on a keyboard.

Drone. A sustained note (or sometimes sustained tonic and dominant notes) against which other parts play or sing melodies, especially in music that shows some folk influence. There is not necessarily any dissonance as there is with a **pedal**.

Du talon. Direction to a string player to use the part of the bow hair nearest to the heel (near where the player holds the bow), producing a stronger, rougher attack.

Échappée. An échappée (or 'escape note') leaves a harmony note by step (usually upwards) and then leaps in the opposite direction (usually by a 3rd) to a new harmony note.

Expressionism. One of the most important musical movements of the 20th century, led by the composers Schoenberg, Berg and Webern. As the name suggests, it applies to music in which a composer's inner turmoil is reflected in unsettled, chaotic music.

False relation. The occurrence of the ordinary and chromatically altered versions of the same note (such as F♯ and F♮) in two different parts at the same time, or in close proximity.

Free jazz. Avant-garde jazz of the 1960s, with a loose approach to tonality, chord sequences and structure.

Fugal. *See* **Fugue**.

Fugue. A type of piece in which a theme called a 'subject' is treated in imitation by all the parts (usually with short passages called 'episodes' from which it is absent, for relief and contrast). The adjective is **fugal** (for instance, 'in fugal style' means 'in the style of a fugue').

Functional harmony. A type of harmony that has the *function* of defining a major or minor key, in particular through chords on the tonic and dominant (I and V$^{(7)}$), with special emphasis on perfect cadences (V$^{(7)}$–I).

Gamelan. An ensemble from Indonesia (usually Bali or Java) consisting largely of tuned percussion.

Genre. A type of music. Genres include the sonata, the string quartet and the symphony.

Glissando. A slide between two notes.

Gongan. In **gamelan** music, a rhythmic unit concluded by the sounding of the Gong.

Gymel. In English vocal music of the late 15th and early 16th centuries, the temporary division of a single voice part (especially the treble part) into two to provide additional fullness or brightness of texture.

Harmonics. A technique of lightly touching a string on a string instrument to produce an artificial high sound (sometimes rather flute-like in sound).

Hemiola. The articulation of two units of triple time (strong–weak–weak, strong–weak–weak) as three units of duple time (strong–weak, strong–weak, strong–weak).

Heterophony. A texture in which a melody is performed simultaneously with one or more rhythmically and/or melodically varied versions of itself.

Homophony. A texture in which one part has a melody and the other parts accompany, in contrast to **contrapuntal** writing, where each part has independent melodic and rhythmic interest.

Imitation. Where a melodic idea in one part is immediately repeated in another part (exactly or inexactly), at the same or a different pitch, while the first part continues. The adjective is 'imitative'.

Imperfect cadence. An open-ended or inconclusive cadence ending with the dominant chord (V). The preceding chord is usually I, ii or IV.

Impressionism. A compositional movement that began in France in the late 19th century and continued into the 20th, and was in some respects similar to the art movement of the same name. Important characteristics of impressionist music include heightened attention to timbre, colour and atmosphere, non-functional harmony and tonality and fluid metre.

Instrumentation. The choice of instruments for a piece of music. (The expression 'instrumental forces' is sometimes used instead.)

Interrupted cadence. A cadence intended to create surprise or suspense, perhaps by delaying the arrival of a final perfect or plagal cadence. Usually an interrupted cadence consists of chord V followed by chord VI.

Inversion. When a chord has a note other than the root in the lowest part, it is an inversion. In a first-inversion chord the 3rd of the chord is the lowest part, and in a second-inversion chord the 5th. For example, a triad of F major in first inversion is A–C–F, and in second inversion is C–F–A.

Ionian mode. A scale that uses the following pattern of tones (T) and semitones (s): T–T–s–T–T–T–s. When starting on C, it consists of all the white notes within one octave on a keyboard.

Isorhythmic. Using a repeating rhythmic pattern in conjunction with the repetition of a pre-existing melody or cantus firmus, the rhythmic pattern and melodic repetition being 'out of phase'.

Keteg. In **gamelan** music, individual rhythmic cells, the equivalent of bars, which together form the **gongan**.

Lied. German for song, but used in English to refer specifically to 19th-century settings of German poetry for an accompanied solo voice.

Lombardic rhythm. A 'reversed' dotted rhythm, with the shorter note first, e.g. semiquaver–dotted quaver. The term 'Scotch snap' is sometimes used instead.

Magnificat. The words of the Virgin Mary before the birth of Jesus (from the gospel of Luke, chapter 1), widely sung in church services, including the Church of England service of Evening Prayer or Evensong. 'Magnificat' is the first word of the Latin version of this song.

Mass. The Mass is the principal act of worship of the Roman Catholic Church; it corresponds in some ways with services of Holy Communion in other churches. The word 'mass' (often, as here, with a lower-case 'm') can also refer to a musical setting of certain texts from the Mass (for example, Gloria in excelsis and Sanctus).

Masque. Form of English court entertainment from the 17th and early 18th centuries – staged, with singing, instrumental music and dancing.

Melisma. In vocal music, a group of notes on a single syllable, often for expressive purposes or word-painting.

Melody-dominated homophony. As with 'ordinary' homophony, a texture in which one part has a melody and the other parts accompany. With melody-dominated homophony, however, the melody stands apart from the accompaniment particularly clearly and strongly.

Metre. Concerns the identity, grouping and subdivision of beats, as indicated by a time signature. E.g. the time signature $\frac{3}{4}$ indicates a simple triple metre, in which each bar consists of three crotchet beats, any of which can be divided into two quavers. In contrast, $\frac{9}{8}$ is a compound triple metre, in which each bar consists of three dotted-crotchet beats, any of which can be divided into three quavers.

Modal. A term often used to refer to music based on a mode rather than on major and minor keys.

Monophony. Music consisting only of a single melodic line. The adjective is 'monophonic'.

Mordent. A quick ornament, denoted by a conventional sign. There is movement from the main (printed or written) note to the note above (upper mordent) or below (lower mordent) and back again.

Motet. A type of church music for choir, sometimes accompanied by organ, and occasionally by larger forces. A motet often has Latin words (commonly from the Bible), and is particularly but not exclusively associated with Roman Catholic services.

Motif. A short but distinctive musical idea that is developed in various ways in order to create a longer passage of music. The adjective is 'motivic' (e.g. 'motivic development' means 'development of a motif').

Neapolitan 6th. A chromatic chord (often in a minor key) consisting of the first inversion of the major chord formed on the flattened supertonic, i.e. the flattened second degree of the scale (in D minor for example, the Neapolitan 6th has the notes G–B♭–E♭).

Neoclassical. A term used for music in which the composer revives elements from an earlier style (not necessarily a Classical one). These elements normally exist alongside more up-to-date ones – mere copying of an old style is 'pastiche'.

Obbligato. A prominent (and essential – 'obligatory') instrumental part in Baroque music, often in an aria, in addition to the vocal part and continuo.

Opera. A large-scale dramatic work for singers and instrumentalists. In most cases the whole text is sung, so that an opera is very different from a play with incidental music. An opera differs from a musical too (for example, the music is not generally popular in idiom).

Oratorio. A large-scale work on a religious subject for solo voice(s), chorus and instruments in a number of movements. *See also* **Cantata**.

Ornamentation. Addition of melodic decoration, often through the use of conventional forms of ornamentation such as **trills** and **mordents**.

Ostinato. A repeating melodic, harmonic or rhythmic motif, heard continuously throughout part or the whole of a piece.

Pedal. A sustained or repeated note, usually in a low register, over which changing harmonies occur. A pedal on the fifth note of the scale (a dominant pedal) tends to create a sense of expectation in advance of a perfect cadence; a pedal on the keynote (a tonic pedal) can create a feeling of repose.

Perfect cadence. A cadence ending with the tonic chord (I), preceded by the dominant (V or V^7) – appropriate where some degree of finality is required.

Pelog. In **gamelan** music, a seven-note scale. Often, as in *Baris Melampahan*, only five notes from such a scale are actually used.

Pentatonic. A scale made up of five notes, most frequently the first, second, third, fifth and sixth degrees of a major scale (for example, the major pentatonic scale of C is C–D–E–G–A).

Phrygian cadence. A type of imperfect cadence, in which the dominant chord (V) is preceded by the first inversion of the subdominant (IVb). It is used chiefly in minor keys, and particularly in Baroque music.

Quartal harmony. Harmony based on the interval of a 4th (e.g. with chords such as A–D–G), rather than on the interval of a 3rd as in triads and 7th chords.

Range. The interval between the lowest note in a passage and the highest (for example, a melody with middle C as the lowest note and C in the third space of the treble stave as highest note has a range of an octave).

Recitative. A piece for solo voice in an opera, cantata or oratorio (often before an **aria**) in which clear projection of words is the main concern. In many recitatives the music is functional rather than of great interest in itself, with the accompaniment often just for continuo.

Relative major and minor. Keys that have the same key signature but a different scale (e.g. F major and D minor, both with a key signature of one flat). A relative minor is three semitones lower than its relative major (e.g. the tonic of D minor is three semitones lower than the tonic of its relative major, F major).

Riff. A short, catchy melodic figure, repeated like an **ostinato** and commonly found in rock, pop and jazz.

Ritornello form. A structure used in Baroque music in which an opening instrumental section (called the ritornello) introduces the main musical ideas. This returns, often in shortened versions and in related keys, between passages for one or more soloists. The complete ritornello (or a substantial part of it) returns in the tonic key at the end.

Rondo. A piece in which an opening section in the tonic key is heard several times, with different material ('episodes'), usually in different keys, between these repetitions. The simplest rondo shape is A B A C A (where A is the recurring section and B and C are episodes), but this can be extended, for instance with additional episode(s) and further repeats of the A section.

Scotch snap. *See* **Lombardic rhythm**.

Sequence. Immediate repetition of a melodic or harmonic idea at a different pitch.

Serial. In serial music all (or most) pitches are derived from an underlying fixed series of pitches that can be manipulated by transposition, inversion and retrograding (being played backwards). A widely practiced form of serialism in the mid 20th century used a series (or 'row') of twelve notes that included every note of the chromatic scale once.

Sonata. An instrumental work, commonly in three or four movements. From the late Baroque period onwards, sonatas are usually for solo keyboard or for single melody instrument and keyboard. 'Trio sonatas' (middle to late Baroque) are normally for two violins and continuo.

Suspension. A suspension occurs at a change of chord, when one part hangs on to (or repeats) a note from the old chord, creating a dissonance, after which the delayed part resolves by step (usually down) to a note of the new chord.

Sustaining pedal. The right pedal on a piano that, while held down, sustains note(s) even after the fingers have been lifted from the keys.

Swing. A popular big-band style mainly of the 1930s. 'Swung rhythms' typically feature pairs of quavers in which the first is lengthened in performance, the second shortened.

Symphony. A work for orchestra with several (usually three or four) movements in different tempi – in effect a sonata for orchestra rather than for one or a few instruments.

Syncopation. The shifting of stress from a strong to a weak beat. For example, in a $\frac{4}{4}$ bar with the rhythm ♩♩♩, the minim (a relatively long note beginning on a weak beat) is syncopated.

Ternary form. A musical structure of three sections in which the outer sections are similar and the central one contrasting (ABA).

Texture. The relationship between the various simultaneous lines in a passage of music, dependent on such features as the number and function of the parts and the spacing between them.

Tierce de Picardie. A major 3rd in the final tonic chord of a passage in a minor key.

Tonality. The system of major and minor keys in which one note (the tonic, or key note) has particular importance, and in which various keys are related. Especially in the 18th and 19th centuries, tonality is established by the use of functional harmony. For exam purposes, questions on tonality might also include indentifying music that is modal (based on one or more modes) or that is based on non-western scales. Western music that uses neither keys nor modes is described as atonal (without tonality).

Tremolo. A rapid and continuous repetition of a single note or two alternating notes.

Trill. An ornament in which two adjacent notes rapidly and repeatedly alternate (the note bearing the trill sign and the one above it). The symbol for a trill is *tr*.

Triplet. A group of three equal notes played in the time normally taken by two notes of the same type. For example, a triplet of quavers is played in the time taken by two normal quavers.

Una corda. The left pedal on a piano, which has a muting effect produced usually by shifting the action so that the hammers strike only one string where there is a group of two or three strings for a note (or strike off-centre where there is only one string).

Vocalisation. A style of singing in which pitches are produced without distinct words. The term often refers to technical exercises for singers that focus on vowels, but composers have written textless vocal pieces for performance.

Whole-tone scale. A scale in which the interval between every successive note is a whole tone.

Edexcel A2 Music Listening Tests scores booklet

Question 2: Aural Awareness (2012)

Test 1 (2012)

Test 2 (2012)

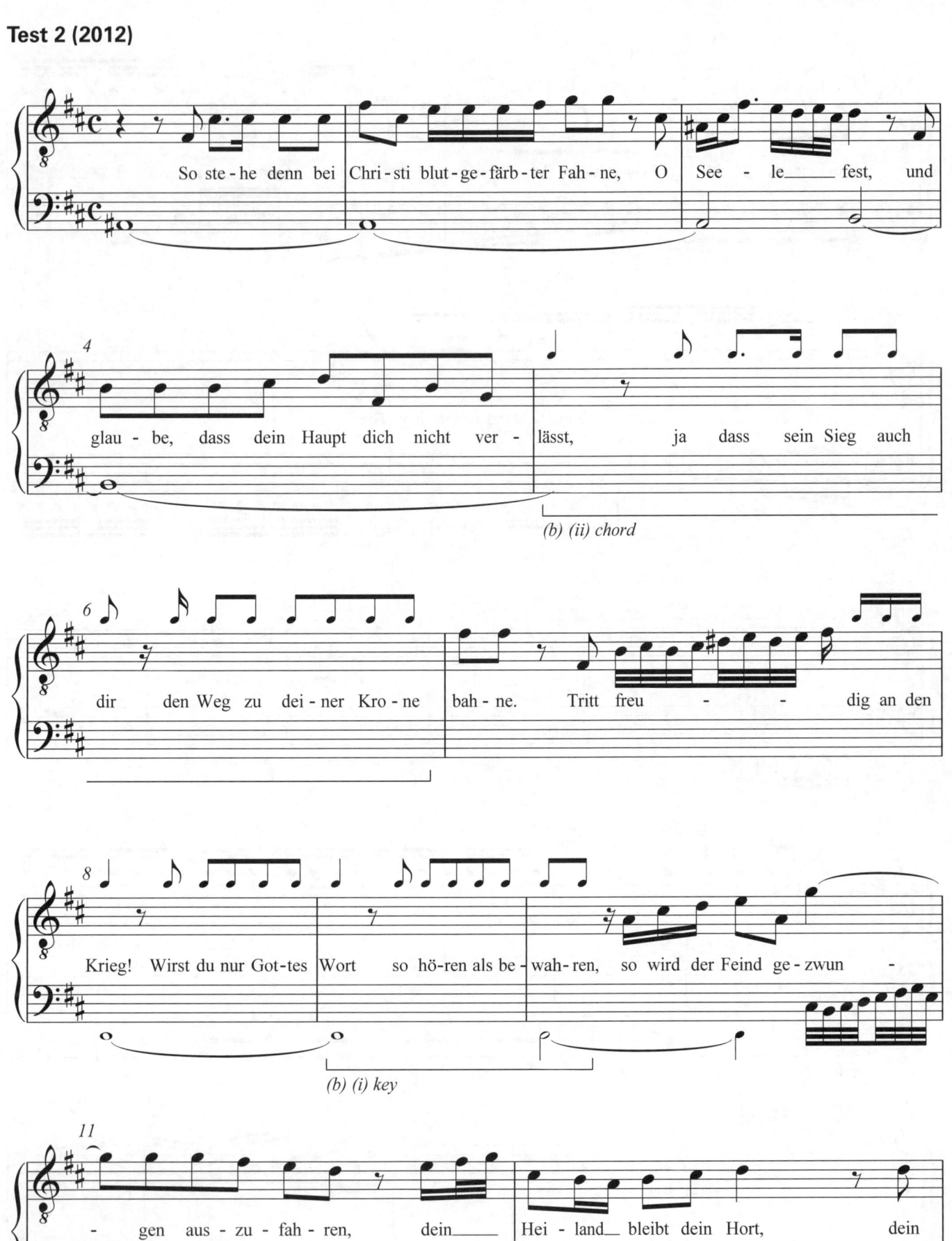

(b) (ii) chord

(b) (i) key

(b) (iii) type of chord

Hei - land__ bleibt dein Hort, dein Hei - land bleibt__ dein__ Hort.__

_____ dein Hei-land bleibt dein Hort.

(b) (iv) cadence

(b) (v) dissonance

(b) (i) key

Translation:

So stand by Christ's blood-spattered banner, my soul, and trust in his everlasting protection.
Yes, he will help you gain your crown of victory.
Go forth joyously to the fight!
If you hear God's word, and do as he commands, no foe will prevail against you,
your salvation will be sure and your refuge secure.
Blessed is he who praises God.

Test 3 (2012)

Test 4 (2012)

Question 2: Aural Awareness (2013)

Test 1 (2013)

(b) (iv) key?

(b) (iv) key?

Test 2 (2013)

Translation:

Blessed is he who comes in the name of the Lord.

Test 3 (2013)

Test 4 (2014)